D1600059

DAILY COMPANION
FOR CAREGIVERS

"When he saw him, he was moved with compassion."
—Lk 10:33

DAILY COMPANION FOR CAREGIVERS

MINUTE MEDITATIONS FOR EVERY DAY CONTAINING A SCRIPTURE OR INSPIRATIONAL READING, A REFLECTION, AND A PRAYER

By
Allan F. Wright

CATHOLIC BOOK PUBLISHING CORP.
New Jersey

CONTENTS

NIHIL OBSTAT: Rev. Stephen Prisk, S.T.L.
Censor Librorum

IMPRIMATUR: ✚ Most Rev. Arthur J. Serratelli, S.T.D., S.S.L., D.D.
Bishop of Paterson

July 18, 2018

The Nihil Obstat and Imprimatur are official declarations that a book or a pamphlet is free of doctrinal or moral error. No implication is contained therein that those who have granted the Nihil Obstat and Imprimatur agree with the contents, opinions or statements expressed.

(T-161)

ISBN 978-1-947070-27-1

© 2018 Catholic Book Publishing Corp., N.J.
Printed in Korea
www.catholicbookpublishing.com

INTRODUCTION

At every age and every stage of our lives caregivers play an important role. They affect the lives of others for the better. What a great legacy to leave behind! Caregivers come in all shapes, sizes, and ages, and some are caregivers by nature while others through their profession. For those who enter a career where serving others is first and foremost, opportunities abound to serve and provide care for others often when those they serve are at their weakest or in most need.

What difference does it make that a caregiver is a person of faith? I believe faith in Jesus makes a profound difference. Not that those without the gift of faith perform with less professionalism than those with faith, but as Catholics we have a sacramental view of the world, of life, of people. We believe that whatsoever we do to the least of these people, we do for Christ. The manner and patience in which we teach, the small things done with great love, all reflect a fundamental belief that every person and every action when given over to God has eternal effects. What a joy it is to serve and care for others with this divine perspective.

Those who are caregivers also need to care for themselves. They are often on the front lines of service tending to the needs of students, patients, the community, family, and beyond. In their effort to care for others some tend to forget and neglect care for themselves in the midst of their labor.

This "Daily Companion" is to be an encouragement for those who provide care as well as an exhortation to continue to be the "light of the world" and the presence of Christ to others through how we care and love one another. St. Paul reminds us that in the end there are three things that matter: faith, hope, and love, and the greatest of these is love. For love to be real it must be put into action and those who care for others do just that in the providence of their daily lives.

As a husband to a wonderful wife and father to four children I see ample opportunities to both serve and care for my family in the simplicity of our humble home. I hope that your caring for others begins at home and that your children and loved ones replicate your witness of caring for that is the only legacy that matters.

Allan F. Wright
Feast of St. André Besette, C.S.C.
January 6

WAS hungry and you gave me food, I was thirsty and you gave me drink. —Mt 25:35

JAN. 1

You are the presence of Christ

REFLECTION. Many people believe that they need to join a religious order or take a service trip to a Third World country in order to fulfill these words of Christ. Not true!

Joining together with others to feed the hungry is a way to multiply our efforts, but don't forget that opportunities often lie at our own doorstep.

PRAYER. *Jesus, may I see Your face in those I feed—family, friends, others.*

 HATEVER you did for one of these least brothers of mine, you did for me. —Mt 25:40

JAN. 2

God needs your loving witness

REFLECTION. Not that God can't do miracles without us but throughout the Scriptures God chooses to ask for help.

From Abraham to Moses to Rahab to Mary and the prophets and the men and women of the New Testament, God allows us to participate in His work. Imagine the welcome you will receive in Heaven for helping to serve God's people.

PRAYER. *Lord God, give me the strength to say "Yes" to caring for others.*

EHOLD, I stand at the door and knock.
—Rev 3:20

Knocking at the door of our heart

REFLECTION. The invitation from Jesus is for all, saints and sinners alike. The degree to which we open the door is the degree to which we will experience the joy of Jesus.

In opening the door and letting Jesus in we will discover that His will includes service to others. Maybe it will be our vocation to serve in the health field, but we all will have some small part to do.

PRAYER. *Merciful Lord, I accept Your invitation to be Lord of my life and to serve.*

 OAH complied, just as the Lord had commanded.
—Gen 7:5

Caregivers need care as well

REFLECTION. When serving others consumes our life and becomes the focus of everything, we can begin to lose focus and neglect our loved ones and ourselves.

Take time each day for prayer, family, and friends so that you will be able to serve as a healthy person. What activities bring you joy? Which people give you life?

PRAYER. *Mary, Mother of God, remind me to slow down and to spend time with friends.*

HAVE the strength for everything through him who empowers me. —Phil 4:13

Let Jesus work through you

REFLECTION. The fortitude and courage that many caregivers possess is amazing. Often it is they who model the compassion of Jesus.

Remember that Jesus sees and realizes the sacrifices you make each and every day, and your service brings a smile to His holy face. When you feel unnoticed and fed up with life, remember Jesus knows.

PRAYER. *Jesus, may I serve with a joyful heart no matter who is around to see me.*

EING present when someone is suffering has given my life new meaning.
—Dana Flynn, R.N.

Suffering can take many forms

REFLECTION. Nurses have always played a special part in the lives of patients and families for they are on the front lines when there is suffering and difficult decisions to make.

Nurses are often behind the scenes making their late night rounds and going through a litany of monotonous but necessary tasks to ensure the proper care of their patients. Doing those small things with great love makes all the difference.

PRAYER. *Jesus, may I give my patients proper care and support at every stage of their illness.*

LESSED are they who mourn, for they will be comforted. —Mt 5:4

What do we "mourn" over?

REFLECTION. Only in Heaven will we experience perpetual joy and happiness. We obviously experience joy on earth, but we must learn to accept suffering as part of God's plan too.

It may seem strange that God allows suffering, but we remember that Jesus wept at the loss of His friend Lazarus and He faced incredible suffering on the Cross. God, however, has a perfect plan.

PRAYER. *Lord, let me not lose sight of Your faithfulness in times of suffering.*

———————

ND behold, I am with you always, until the end of the age. —Mt 28:20

He goes with you

REFLECTION. It can be extremely difficult to be a caregiver and the fact is that some of those you care for may not have the mental capacity to appreciate what you are doing for them.

Regardless of how others respond, those who care continue to serve because in serving others they serve God in their fellow man.

PRAYER. *Lord, give me strength to serve even when my service isn't recognized or appreciated.*

EVER underestimate the power of a smile, a kind word, or a loving touch.
—Dr. Steve Demcsak

JAN.
9

Sound advice from a doctor

REFLECTION. Medical professionals spend years studying their area of expertise and thousands upon thousands of dollars to receive their degrees. Thank God for their dedication to their profession.

They realize, of course, that they don't treat diseases, they treat people. In treating the whole person, the care they give in a smile and in kind words help in the healing process.

PRAYER. *Jesus, may I never forget the "small" things that can change someone's day.*

———

 T'S an honor to care for someone who cared for us.
—Sarah Ceteras, P.A.

JAN.
10

Time to give back

REFLECTION. Caring for an elderly parent presents a number of challenges for adult children. The physical, financial, and emotional needs can be overwhelming. Yet, caring for one who cared for us is indeed an honor.

When caring for someone who cared for us becomes challenging remember that we are here to serve as Jesus served.

PRAYER. *Lord, may the moments I spend with an aging parent be filled with moments of grace.*

11

ELOVED, let us love one another, because love is of God. —1 Jn 4:7

You are an agent of God's love

REFLECTION. Most people who are considered saints are the first to balk at that suggestion for they realize their own faults and failings.

While some people are officially canonized Saints in the Church, all who are baptized are called to live as witnesses to the love of God in their lives. The proof that we are saints is that we love one another.

PRAYER. *Lord God, thank You for loving me as I am.*

 OVE seeks one thing only: the good of the one loved. —Thomas Merton

God loves you!

REFLECTION. Caregivers are so often giving of themselves that they tend to forget that they are loved for who they are and not for what they do. Sometimes we may feel we need to earn God's love but this is not the Gospel.

The love of God is received as a free gift. How do you receive that love? Take some time to reflect on God's personal love for you.

PRAYER. *Loving God, may my service to others be a result of being overwhelmed by Your love.*

BLESSED be the God and Father of our Lord Jesus Christ, the Father of mercy and the God of all encouragement.
—2 Cor 1:3

JAN.
13

God is cheering for us

REFLECTION. When St. Paul begins his letter to the Corinthians his focus is on God. St. Paul then describes two of God's attributes which he wants to highlight for the Christians in Corinth. The two qualities are compassion and encouragement.

When you are feeling drained and at the end of your wits remember that God is cheering for you.

PRAYER. *Lord, I'm glad that You are on my side each and every step of my journey.*

GOD consoles us in all our afflictions and enables us to console others in their tribulations.
—2 Cor 1:4

JAN.
14

Pay it forward

REFLECTION. They say we only know how to give what we receive. Those who never receive love or mercy may find it difficult to show love and mercy to others.

As disciples of Jesus we have received not only these gifts but the power to live them out even in the most difficult of circumstances through the empowerment of the Holy Spirit.

PRAYER. *Come, Holy Spirit, Comforter and Counselor, empower me when I am at my weakest.*

S O THROUGH Christ does our encouragement also overflow. —2 Cor 1:5

JAN. 15

Let God's love flow over you

REFLECTION. Some would have us believe that we are insignificant in light of the enormity of the universe. But our faith reveals another story. That story is one where every action done out of love is not only significant but in fact, eternal.

When you need some down time let Jesus know how you feel in any way that you're comfortable with and then be silent.

PRAYER. *Mary, Mother of God, be a mother to me as I serve those around me.*

T HE burden we endured was far too heavy for us to bear, so that we even despaired of life. — 2 Cor 1:8

JAN. 16

From the mouth of St. Paul

REFLECTION. We can forget that even the Saints had difficulty in their life and at times were prone to despair. Fortunately, these men and women had strong faith.

Faith enables us to believe in God's grace and timing in even the most troubling of circumstances. Realize that during the valleys of life God is with you each and every step.

PRAYER. *Lord God, may I never give in to despair and may Your Holy Spirit comfort me.*

HE DELIVERED us from this deadly peril, and he will continue to rescue us.

—2 Cor 1:10

God came to save us

REFLECTION. What St. Paul learned from his trials is that God is indeed faithful in all matters great and small.

As a caregiver there are great and small ways that you bring healing and relief, peace and mercy. Trust in God's provision for you and be thankful for those times where you have been God's presence.

PRAYER. *Lord Jesus, thank You for saving me from sin and for being my savior.*

IT'S rewarding and challenging to be on the scene when people suffer and need help.

—Richard Costanza, Police Officer

One shift at a time

REFLECTION. Ninety percent of the time that the police are involved in people's lives is when there is a crisis. This is not surprising and the police know what they are getting into when they sign up.

The challenge for those in law enforcement where every move is questioned and challenged is to see every human being as a reflection of God. This is not a human, but superhuman achievement.

PRAYER. *Come Holy Spirit, empower me to serve others with a pure heart.*

FOR we are indeed the aroma of Christ to God among those who are being saved.

—2 Cor 2:15

The fragrance of Christ

REFLECTION. When the Romans conquered a city they would lead a procession of their captives in chains before the army. Leading everyone would be soldiers who had a huge cauldron of fragrant incense. Those who smelled it knew it was the smell of victory.

When you walk throughout your day connected to Christ, you too, walk in victory and reflect the love of God in Jesus.

PRAYER. *Christ the King, remind me of my victory over sin through the sacrifice of Jesus.*

WHEN the airbag drops in the airplane, care for yourself and then care for others.

—Pam Weller, Flight Attendant

Self-care is smart care

REFLECTION. Those in the "caring industry" are constantly pulled in many directions. Their ability to multi-task is amazing and sometimes they begin to think they themselves are the savior of the world.

This type of thinking can lead to an unhealthy lifestyle where they are exhausted and prone to sickness. Schedule "down time" and take care of yourself in order to be able to serve others.

PRAYER. *Lord, I commit to making time for prayer and my spiritual life each day.*

THEREFORE, since we have such hope, **JAN.**
we act with complete confidence.
—2 Cor 3:12 **21**

Act boldly in love

REFLECTION. One of the attributes of caregivers is that when it's time to act they act. Even when the patient may not want the medicine the caregiver knows what's best.

God is the ultimate caregiver and He commands that we have a "Sabbath" each week. It may be a bold move to take a day off each week to spend in worship, with family, and for relaxation, but the Chief caregiver commands it.

PRAYER. *Abba, Father, may my actions of love be bold and frequent.*

FOR the Lord watches over the way of the **JAN.**
righteous. —Ps 1:6 **22**

God is aware of your sacrifice

REFLECTION. People who serve out of love don't count the cost. There are those times when we ask the question, "Is it all worth it?" The Catholic answer is a resounding "YES."

No act of love or service is ever wasted in the eyes of God, no matter how small it may be. When you are tempted to get down on yourself or life, remember His abundant love.

PRAYER. *Jesus, save me from despair when life and service seem too difficult to continue.*

BLESSED are all those who take refuge in him. —Ps 2:11

JAN.
23

God is our hiding place

REFLECTION. The word "blessed" is found many times in the Bible and often on the lips of Jesus. It is a state of being holy or sanctified. It is a present reality rather than a future promise which means that we experience the blessing right now.

Often we work to achieve a future goal or reward and fail to realize that God is present now. Find time to take refuge in God today.

PRAYER. *Lord, may I see Your blessings in my life and be thankful for every one of them.*

SO MUCH of what we do is preparation. When we are needed, we are ready to act. —Rich Hernandez, Firefighter

JAN.
24

Prepared and ready

REFLECTION. Years of education and training go into the formation of professional caregivers and rescue workers. The time spent studying and training can seem tedious when the chances of a fire or disaster are relatively rare.

Thanks be to God for those who do give it their all and are prepared for the worst case scenario anytime and anyplace.

PRAYER. *Lord, protect those who put themselves in harm's way to protect others.*

HENEVER I cry aloud to the Lord, he answers me from his holy mountain. —Ps 3:5

How does God answer?

REFLECTION. The author of the Psalms is very confident that God has not only heard his prayer but answers it as well. What would it be like to have that same confidence?

God does indeed answer but not always in the way in which we would like Him to. Pray earnestly and don't be afraid to look for God's answers in unexpected places and through ordinary people. Trust in Him.

PRAYER. *Merciful God, hear my prayers and give me the faith to be persistent.*

ISE up, O Lord! Rescue me, O my God! —Ps 3:8

We can model our Father's love

REFLECTION. Most, if not all, great adventure novels and movies await a savior at the end of the conflict—someone who will rescue the main character from disaster and thus "save the day."

Those who are caregivers come to the rescue of others multiple times each day. In doing so they are modeling and reflecting the care and love that God has for others.

PRAYER. *Jesus, may I imitate You in all of my words and actions.*

T'S both wonderful and challenging to be the caregivers to my grandchildren.
—Hattie Beauregard

JAN. 27

A new role for grandparents

REFLECTION. Many grandparents are being asked to be the caretakers of their grandchildren these days. From dropping them off at school to providing aftercare, grandparents fill the gap in the lives of many working parents.

The beautiful gift of unconditional love that grandparents provide is a reflection of God's unconditional love for us.

PRAYER. *St. Anne and St. Joachim, pray for grandparents that they would provide faith and guidance as you did.*

 EMEMBER that the Lord wonderfully favors those who are faithful. —Ps 4:4

JAN. 28

Focus on faithfulness

REFLECTION. If being faithful was easy then everybody would be faithful, but we know that's not always the case. Jesus knew full well that the cares and worries of this world can overwhelm us and make us lose our focus on God.

If you are one of the faithful who remembers Christ daily in your prayers and action that's great. If not, make time to get back on track.

PRAYER. *Lord Jesus, forgive me for my unfaithfulness and help me to be faithful.*

GROWTH begins when we start to accept our weakness. —Jean Vanier

It takes humility to accept our weaknesses

REFLECTION. Jean Vanier is a Catholic philosopher, theologian, and humanitarian who has a legacy of forming small communities. His insight is key for those who give aid and comfort to others because there is a temptation to believe that we have all the answers and have reached perfection ourselves.

Uncover your heart and embrace those areas in your life where you are weak.

PRAYER. *Lord, in admitting my weaknesses I realize how much more I need You in my life.*

LORD, at daybreak you hear my voice; at daybreak I bring my petition before you. —Ps 5:4

A daily routine

REFLECTION. The author of the Psalms says quite plainly that the Lord hears his voice at daybreak. This suggests both his confidence in the Lord and that he has a daily routine where he lets the Lord know what's going on in his life.

While the Lord already knows our needs, it's good for us to let our petitions be known to God for He asks us to do so.

PRAYER. *Lord God, may my first thoughts each morning be focused on You.*

M Y EYES grow dim because of my grief; they are worn out because of all my foes. —Ps 6:8

Who are your foes?

REFLECTION. Many caregivers have to struggle with keeping grief at bay. The very nature of the work they do will put them in situations where grief and sorrow are close at hand and these can become our enemies, our foes.

This is natural and throughout the Scriptures we read of people who experience grief. Jesus Himself wept openly at the news that His friend Lazarus had died.

PRAYER. *Lord, may my grief be acknowledged and may Your Holy Spirit be with me always.*

Y OU can't pour from an empty cup. —Walter Sobczak

Where is your spiritual well?

REFLECTION. People who constantly give to others need to have someone from whom they can draw strength. For Christians, that source of strength comes from Jesus and from the Christian community.

It can be an act of pride to think that we can go it alone. Make the time to pray and to ask for friends along the way who will support you.

PRAYER. *Mary, Mother of God, be a mother to me as I seek to serve God's people.*

HE Lord is a refuge for the oppressed, a refuge in times of distress. —Ps 9:10

**FEB.
2**

What about me?

REFLECTION. Those who are caregivers may sometimes wonder, "What's in it for me?" It seems we give so much and barely receive any recognition for our labor. At these times we need to turn to the Lord who understands us.

Jesus received praise and adulation but was also scorned by others and crucified. Place your trust in Him who knows how you feel.

PRAYER. *Holy Spirit, empower me and comfort me so I will not feel overwhelmed.*

ARING for my mom who has Alzheimer's has been the biggest challenge in my life. —John Mulvaney

**FEB.
3**

The gift of thankless service

REFLECTION. A few strategies that are relayed by caregivers who work with Alzheimer's patients are: don't argue, redirect conversations; don't try to reason but be sure to reassure them; never lecture.

The advice points to a bigger picture where we need to adjust the way we behave in order to better serve those we care for. In the end, God knows our efforts.

PRAYER. *Lord, when I get frustrated change my heart to serve as You would serve.*

BUT you will receive power when the Holy Spirit comes upon you. —Acts 1:8

Power is available from God

REFLECTION. People who are constantly serving others can feel underappreciated and that can turn to bitterness which does no one any good. What often brings this sense of underappreciation is relying on others for praise and admiration.

Ask for the Holy Spirit to fill you with the love of God and know that God appreciates your service to His people.

PRAYER. *Come Holy Spirit, may God's love overflow into all of my words and actions.*

ALL of these were constantly engaged in prayer, together with the women and Mary the mother of Jesus. —Acts 1:14

Gather together in prayer

REFLECTION. As we read about the life of Jesus and the early community in the New Testament there are moments when Jesus and His disciples gather in prayer.

If it's important for Jesus and the disciples to gather to pray then it's imperative that we gather with others to pray. Their example tells us how important community prayer is, and when we pray together we walk in their footsteps.

PRAYER. *Lord God, may I make communal prayer part of my weekly routine.*

I RELY on the strength of my fellow nurses when a young life is in danger. **FEB. 6**

—Dana Flynn, R.N.

Lean on me

REFLECTION. Most of us have a regular routine that we go through each day and major disruptions are more of the exception than the norm. Some caregivers are in situations where they have no idea what each day will bring.

Be open to the possibility that God has you right where He wants you. You may be the answer to someone who is praying for a miracle. Lean on Him.

PRAYER. *Jesus, give me Your strength and the strength of friends so I can be my best.*

ALL of them were filled with the Holy Spirit and began to speak in different languages. **—Acts 2:4** **FEB. 7**

What's your primary language of love?

REFLECTION. We have the greatest gift available to us that is given by the Father and the Son. This is the Holy Spirit, who empowers us to witness to God's love.

As the early Church spoke in various languages it may be good to reflect on our "love language." At different times it's our words that are loving, or our actions, and always our thoughts and prayers can be expressions of love.

PRAYER. *Blessed Virgin Mary, help me to lovingly receive the Holy Spirit.*

FAITH grows when it is lived and shaped by love. This is why our families, our homes are true domestic churches.

FEB. 8

—Pope Francis

Faith begins at home

REFLECTION. What's the worth of a good lawyer or successful business professional? Surely they are not worth more than a loving, faith-filled mother and father.

With a stable, loving environment the child has a great advantage in becoming the man or woman God has called them to be. Pray for families and parents.

PRAYER. *St. Joseph, may my family be a place of faith and support centered on Jesus Christ.*

I SAW the Lord always before me; with him at my right hand I shall not be shaken.

FEB. 9

—Acts 2:25

Neither shaken nor stirred

REFLECTION. When trouble and tragedy arrive we can easily take our focus off the Lord and let fear and despair move in. King David faced many troubles yet was always able to return to the Lord. Even in his sin he knew that repentance was the way to re-focus on the Lord.

Choose to focus on Jesus in good times and especially in times of difficulty.

PRAYER. *Lord, may I run to You when I'm afraid and never forget You when the problem subsides.*

IN HER own life Mary completed the pilgrimage of faith, following in the footsteps of her son. —Pope Francis

FEB. 10

You have a pilgrimage of faith to complete

REFLECTION. Vacation time is precious. It's something that we don't want to waste so most people carefully plan their time off down to the smallest detail.

The life of faith is also precious although by the very nature of following Jesus we may not always know where it will take us. Trust Jesus, pray, and follow the Lord's footsteps.

PRAYER. *Jesus, help me to follow especially when my path is not clear.*

———————

THEY devoted themselves to the teaching of the apostles and to the communal fellowship, to the breaking of bread and to prayers. —Acts 2:42

FEB. 11

What or who are you devoted to?

REFLECTION. The early Christians did not have a road map all laid out for them on how to proceed in spreading the Good News of Jesus. As a caregiver our road is not always clear.

Take a page from the first Christians and devote yourself to the teaching of the Church, prayer, fellowship, and most importantly the Eucharist.

PRAYER. *Lord, keep me close to You and Your Church so I may more faithfully serve Your people.*

27

SENSE of awe was felt by all for many wonders and signs were performed by the apostles. —Acts 2:43

You are a wonderworker

REFLECTION. The words "signs and wonders" are often interpreted as "miracles" in the Bible. Signs and wonders seem more within our grasp rather than considering ourselves "miracle workers."

Consider, however, your many actions which are indeed signs and wonders that point to God's presence. Each prayer, each selfless act is a sign of God's love.

PRAYER. *Merciful Lord, use me each day to be a sign and wonder of Your love for others.*

UT Peter said, "I have neither silver nor gold, but what I have I give you." —Acts 3:6

Give what you have

REFLECTION. The miraculous power Jesus possessed was always used for the service of others. The gifts and talents you have should also be used in the same way.

How are you using His gifts? It's good to stop and reflect once in a while, if only to thank God for the gifts we have been given and the chance to use them.

PRAYER. *Thank You, Jesus for all the opportunities to use my gifts in Your service.*

ENLISTED as a Marine to serve my country and to protect the freedom of others.
—William Beauregard, USMC

FEB.
14

Thank God for those who serve in our military

REFLECTION. Military service offers a very concrete way to put our ideals into practice. It's easy to speak about freedom, liberty, and independence and quite another to put our lives on the line for what we believe.

Thank God for those who choose to serve no matter what job they have within the military. Whenever you can, thank those who serve for their service.

PRAYER. *Lord, may I never take for granted the price paid by others for our freedom.*

 THE apostles gave him the name Barnabas, meaning "son of encouragement."
—Acts 4:36

FEB.
15

Service through our words

REFLECTION. If people were to name you by one of your most prominent characteristics, hopefully it wouldn't be; "she who gossips" or "he who is lazy!"

How affirming it was to this man named Joseph that the apostles renamed him "Barnabas" because he was so encouraging.

PRAYER. *Jesus, may I be more encouraging of others, even those who I may not like.*

ETER and the other apostles replied, "We must obey God rather than men."

—Acts 5:29

FEB. 16

Who will you serve?

REFLECTION. Service sometimes comes with a cost. Unlike the apostles it may not involve sacrificing our physical lives to the point of death, but it can cost our time and even friendships.

Like the Good Samaritan who gave his oil, wine, money, and time to the injured man, Jesus knows of your sacrifices. Serve and like Jesus, don't count the cost.

PRAYER. *Lord, may my actions be governed by Your words and example whatever the cost.*

 FEEL that my house becomes a small emergency room whenever sickness strikes our family.

—Trisha LaVar

FEB. 17

Home as a source of comfort and care

REFLECTION. Any mother knows that when the stomach bug strikes one child the rest of the family will follow soon after. Hopefully, Mommy doesn't get sick and the hours tending to the kids aren't prolonged. Some mothers admit that daddy can be the worst patient.

You don't need to travel too far to serve the sick and poor for often they are in our homes.

PRAYER. *Lord, may our family be filled with caregivers who support one another in times of illness.*

ND every day, both in the temple and at home, they never stopped teaching and proclaiming Jesus as the Christ.
—Acts 5:42

FEB.
18

How do we proclaim Christ?

REFLECTION. The task of "proclaiming Christ" may seem reserved for priests and nuns or for those "holy rollers" that can sometimes annoy us with their forceful proclamations.

The truth is that all baptized Catholics are called to proclaim the love and forgiveness of God. This can be done through our words and through our actions.

PRAYER. *Jesus, may my voice and life be a reflection of Your love in and through me.*

We are all in this together

REFLECTION. The early Christians had a problem and it was a good problem. As the community grew they had to determine who would serve at table, who would teach, and who would be sent on a mission. One Church with many ministries.

While your area of service may not be directly with the Church, you are a part of the body of Christ and important to the bigger picture.

PRAYER. *Lord, help me to discern my particular role in serving You and to do it well.*

31

N HOSPICE I have learned more about living than dying. On my headstone it will say, "Make the most of your time on earth."

FEB. 20

—Cindy Hinders Rohrbach, Hospice Nurse

Making the most of life

REFLECTION. What a gift it is to families to have those who work for hospice caring for their loved ones. While hospice workers are confronted with death, the insight given above gives everyone a reason to reflect.

Through the ups and downs of life may you continue to be a ray of light to those who need hope and faith as you serve others with love.

PRAYER. *Jesus, stay close to me as I stay close to those who are near death and dying.*

 ARENTS are the primary educators of the faith. —*Familiaris Consortio*

FEB. 21

Live and share your faith

REFLECTION. Imagine if parents could talk about their faith with the same ease and joy that they speak of their favorite vacation spots or restaurant or even sports teams.

Why don't we speak of our faith? Most likely it's because we rarely saw our own parents speak of faith. We can serve our children by sharing and living out our faith with ease and joy leading them to Heaven in the process.

PRAYER. *Lord, help me break the cycle of silence when it comes to my faith in You.*

NLY to one who loves children may they be entrusted.

—Blessed Pauline Von Mallinckrodt

Love is the key

REFLECTION. Blessed Pauline knew that the key ingredient for those who teach children was love. That's true for any successful person. We must love those we serve.

When we do love those we serve it doesn't feel like work but it's more of a vocation, a way of life which brings us joy. A little knowledge and a love for others is the key to joyful service.

PRAYER. *Lord, may my love for You overflow in my service to others.*

ORD, do not hold this sin against them.

—Acts 7:60

Learning from the master

REFLECTION. This quote certainly seems like it comes from the lips of Jesus, but it comes from the Church's first martyr, St. Stephen.

We don't know if St. Stephen knew Jesus during our Lord's public ministry, but we can tell from his words that he became a disciple at some point for his words are the same as the Lord's. By knowing the Lord we can imitate Him each day.

PRAYER. *Jesus, may my actions of mercy and forgiveness be like Jesus.*

HEN they arrived there, they prayed for them that they might receive the Holy Spirit. —Acts 8:15

The Spirit of the Lord

REFLECTION. As the Church grew, more and more people learned about Jesus. Many who believed in Jesus had not yet received the Holy Spirit who enables us to live the life of service that God calls us to.

Living like Jesus and serving as He did is a supernatural act and in order to do so we need the power that God gives us freely in the Spirit.

PRAYER. *Come Holy Spirit, empower me to serve others as Jesus did with power and joy.*

 AUL, Saul, why are you persecuting me? —Acts 9:4

The conversion of Saul

REFLECTION. St. Paul was not always a saint. (His previous name was Saul.) Fortunately for us, we know that every sinner has a future and God's mercy extends to all people.

It's interesting that Jesus so identifies with His people that when Saul persecutes the Church Jesus says, "why are you persecuting me?" It must be the same when we serve God's people that we are serving Jesus.

PRAYER. *Lord, may I see Your face in all those I serve, even those who don't believe in You.*

Y LIFE as a religious sister gives me the chance to serve Christ through serving others. —Sr. M. Assunta

Who do you not love?

REFLECTION. Jesus makes it very clear that we are to "'love our enemies." While it's quite easy to love those who love us, loving those who we find offensive is really the litmus test of what we believe.

When we do come across someone who is difficult to love remember the words of Jesus and see it as an opportunity to find common ground and reveal the love of Jesus to them.

PRAYER. *Lord, open my eyes to extend Your love to those who I find difficult to love.*

 OWEVER, Barnabas took him and brought him to the apostles.
—Acts 9:27

Who can you bring to Christ?

REFLECTION. It was Barnabas who introduced St. Paul to the apostles. They were afraid of him due to his violent persecution of Christians, but Barnabas bridged the gap and thus the Church was to gain one of its most effective evangelists.

How have you "bridged the gap" in your walk of faith?

PRAYER. *Lord, may I seek opportunities to tell others about my encounter with You.*

HE history of mankind, the history of salvation, passes by way of the family.
—St. John Paul II

FEB. 28

Service begins at home

REFLECTION. The miracle and conversion stories of the Saints are truly amazing. It seems at times that a few of the Saints spent more time serving the poor than attending to their family.

Perhaps the biographers weren't focused on the Saints' family activity, but as St. John Paul II recognized, the faith-filled family is God's instrument for the sanctity of the world.

PRAYER. *Jesus, may I see my family as the most important place for me to begin to serve.*

 ERVING as a mother means waking up with a few goals in mind; to see my son laugh, smile, and learn something new.
—Melissa Dobbin Gennaro

FEB. 29

Everyday goals

REFLECTION. It can be the simple things in life that are the most important especially with small children. While we may hope our child is the next Einstein or Michael Jordan, those things have a way of working themselves out.

What are a few attainable goals that you have for your children? Happy children become happy, well-adjusted adults.

PRAYER. *Lord, may I stop over-planning my children's life and take time to appreciate the small things with them.*

ERVING as a mother means living Jesus' words at the Last Supper: "This is my body, given up for you."

—Lindsay Schlegel, Mother and author

MAR.

1

A joyful sacrifice

REFLECTION. It is said that angels are jealous of humans because we have bodies and angels are disembodied beings. This means that we can smile, embrace each other, and use the gift of our bodies as an expression of love.

Mother's know that their bodies are given over to another, a small wonderful life, which God has entrusted to her and her husband from the moment of conception.

PRAYER. *Lord, I gladly give up my body for the life of my children as You gave Your life for me.*

———————

ETER sent them all out and knelt down and prayed. —Acts 9:40

MAR.

2

Take time alone for yourself

REFLECTION. St. Peter entered a room where a woman lay dead. St. Peter did what he saw the Lord do on many occasions: he sent everyone out of the room, knelt down, and prayed.

There are times when we need to be present to others, and there is a time to be alone and to pray. This is not selfish, it is necessary in order for us to make sure we don't lose ourselves.

PRAYER. *Jesus, may my actions imitate Yours, and may I not be afraid to have time alone!*

TO BE a mom means expecting the unexpected on a daily basis.
—Lindsay Schelgel, Mother and author

Who knows what each day will bring?

REFLECTION. When we are young we live with
the illusion that we can be in control of everything. Without a spouse and children we can
schedule our day and life with some assured-
ness that we can do it all.

When children arrive we know for certain
that we are not in control. See the unexpected as
God's reminder that He is in control, and be
open to what each day brings.

PRAYER. *Lord, remind me that You are with me
when my plans go awry and I get flustered.*

IT WAS in Antioch that the disciples were
first called Christians.   —Acts 11:26

Known for their love for one another

REFLECTION. Those who are in positions of
service are expected to serve for that is their
job. For Catholics the question becomes not
"do you serve?" but "how do you serve?"

In Antioch the followers of Jesus were so like
the Lord that people called them Christians.
This week review how you serve those God has
put in your life and appreciate that God has
placed you in that situation.

PRAYER. *Jesus, guide me in all ways that my
actions may reflect Your love for me.*

THE majority of the work I do is behind the scenes, few people realize my efforts. —Teddy Overman

MAR. 5

Silent servers behind the scenes

REFLECTION. Not everyone who serves receives rounds of applause and attention for what they do. Big conferences and gatherings need people to set up the chairs, get the coffee ready, and make sure everything runs smoothly.

The next time an event runs smoothly, take the time to thank the people who serve wholeheartedly behind the scenes.

PRAYER. *God our Father, remind me that no act of service is insignificant in Your eyes.*

THE beginning of love is to let those we love be perfectly themselves. —Thomas Merton

MAR. 6

Let love be unconditional

REFLECTION. There is always a temptation to hold back our love for others until they meet our expectations. When Jesus ate with the tax collector Zacchaeus He showed him unconditional love and that love transformed this known sinner into a disciple of Christ.

There is no doubt that God will provide opportunities for you to show this type of love on a daily basis with difficult people.

PRAYER. *Lord, allow me the grace to love others as they are as You do.*

39

ECOGNIZING Peter's voice, she was so
overjoyed that, instead of opening the
door, she ran in with the news.

MAR.

7

—Acts 12:14

The sound of your voice

REFLECTION. There are amazing videos recording the reaction of people in comas to a loved one's voice. Sometimes they respond with facial expressions or a squeeze of the hand.

Consider how many people rejoice at the sound of your voice. Knowing that you are present means the world to many people. Your voice can be the sound of hope.

PRAYER. *Jesus, may I be attentive to Your voice that is affirming and full of mercy.*

ND the disciples were filled with joy
and with the Holy Spirit. —Acts 13:52

MAR.

8

What are you filled with?

REFLECTION. Throughout the book of Acts we read that the disciples were filled with both joy and the Holy Spirit. These two attributes go hand in hand. The Holy Spirit empowers us to live and love like Jesus and to show mercy and forgiveness even to those who dislike us.

When you lack joy ask the Holy Spirit to fill and empower you so that you can be the presence of God to others.

PRAYER. *Holy Spirit, come into my life today so I may spread the love of God to others.*

COMPASSION asks us to go where it hurts, to enter into the places of pain, to share in brokenness, fear, confusion, and anguish. —Henri Nouwen

Thank you for your service

REFLECTION. The great gift of caregivers is that they are sensitive to the needs of others and have the courage to do something about those needs. It's one thing to identify a need and another to be part of the solution.

A caregiver's presence communicates in a real and tangible way the love of God to those they serve.

PRAYER. *Jesus, thank You for those who have entered into my pain and are a source of comfort.*

NO ONE has the right to sit down and feel hopeless. There is too much work to do. —Dorothy Day

You are part of the solution

REFLECTION. Make sure that you take care of yourself and have some friends who can encourage you along the way. Stay connected to God through prayer, silence, Scripture, and the sacraments—especially the Eucharist—because there is always more to do.

The good news is that you are part of the solution for many people who need the faith, hope, and love that you provide.

PRAYER. *Guardian angel, protect me from feelings of hopelessness and despair.*

E SHOULD not make things more difficult for the Gentiles who are turning to God. —Acts 15:19

A return to God

REFLECTION. The early Church had a problem which was a good problem: many people were seeking to turn to God. The community, after prayer and discussion, decided to make it easy for the Gentiles to turn to God.

While our Catholic faith has beliefs and commandments, we should never make it difficult for people to turn to God. Keep the faith simple and focus on the essentials.

PRAYER. *Jesus, may I know the faith and share it freely so others can know Your love.*

BOUT midnight, Paul and Silas were praying and singing hymns of praise to God. —Acts 16:25

Prayer and joy in a dire situation

REFLECTION. Paul and Silas having shared the Good News in Asia are rewarded by being arrested and imprisoned. While many people would be understandably distraught, these two Saints are praying and singing to God!

In the most challenging of situations do we have the perspective of Paul and Silas? God is in charge, praise Him!

PRAYER. *Jesus, help me to raise my voice in prayer and song even in dire situations.*

Y CHILDREN will live a legacy that my husband and I have modeled through our marriage.
—Hattie Beauregard

MAR. 13

Service through a good example

REFLECTION. Faith is more "caught" than "taught." The example of a healthy marriage can have ramifications for generations. The way husbands and wives talk to and serve each other are noticed by their children.

Children in turn, usually replicate these actions in their own lives. Be grateful for the positive examples of healthy married couples.

PRAYER. *St. Joseph, help our marriage reflect God's presence in our lives.*

EING a police officer means that I, and my family, make sacrifices so others can be helped.
—Officer Tommy Bell

MAR. 14

Putting their life on the line

REFLECTION. Jesus said that there is no greater love than laying down one's life for one's friends. Police officers lay down their lives each day for total strangers and even for those who protest against them.

Their motivation is more than a paycheck and comes from a conviction that they are called to serve all people and that law and order matter. Pray for the police and their families.

PRAYER. *St. Michael, patron Saint of police officers, watch over and protect them as they serve.*

UDE, a servant of Jesus Christ, and the brother of James. — Jude 1:12

How are you known to others?

REFLECTION. The identity of Jude is somewhat a mystery but most identify him with the apostle named Jude Thaddeus. He was therefore an apostle, a companion of Jesus, and an author of a letter in the New Testament. However, he identifies himself first and foremost as a servant.

Whatever career we have or occupation we choose there will be opportunities to serve others. Do you see yourself as a servant?

PRAYER. *Jesus, may I never be ashamed to be a servant to those You put in my life.*

———————

 AY mercy, peace, and love be granted you in abundance. —Jude 2

The abundant life

REFLECTION. Rarely, if ever, does a person on their deathbed wish they spent more time at the office. The things that make the most difference in life are not things but people and relationships.

As a person who cares for others, think of all the people that you have been a source of mercy, peace, and love for. Rejoice that God has used you to bring some hope in this world.

PRAYER. *Lord God, may I stay focused on those relationships which are life-giving.*

E ALL need a St. Paul and St. Timothy in our life.
—Roger Wilkin, Grandfather

Spiritual direction

REFLECTION. St. Paul called St. Timothy his "spiritual child." This means that St. Paul took young Timothy under his wing and taught him the faith. In a sense he "discipled" Timothy.

We all need a person to help us and encourage us along the way as well as someone that we can take under our wings to show them the way. Who has been your St. Paul? Who is your St. Timothy?

PRAYER. *Heavenly Father, may I use my wisdom to disciple others.*

TART where you can start.
—Dr. Sandro Morales

Let's get this started

REFLECTION. There are always reasons why a project doesn't get off the ground. While excuses abound, we who serve are often called to do the impossible.

The important thing is to get started where you can with what resources you have. It's amazing the progress a few committed people can make, and before they know it. . . miracles happen.

PRAYER. *Jesus, may I keep focused on doing what I can rather than getting discouraged.*

45

THESE godless persons pervert the grace of our God.
—Jude 4

MAR.
19

Through the eyes of faith

REFLECTION. The phrase "godless persons" is one that we don't hear much of these days. It seems pretty strange to refer to a person as "godless." However, much of our society has forgotten the Lord and view the world through a different lens than Christians do.

What keeps you focused on your faith? How do you keep your Christian perspective when serving others in a secular world?

PRAYER. *Jesus, the temptations are many. Help me to see others as You see them through the lens of love.*

———————————

T IS these people who create divisions, who follow their natural instincts and do not possess the Spirit.
—Jude 19

MAR.
20

The Holy Spirit empowers us

REFLECTION. One of the main tactics of the devil is to divide and separate people. These divisions tend to grow over time if not resolved quickly.

We can be tempted to see others not as our brothers and sisters but as somehow different and not deserving of our care. Rise above the temptation to put others into categories, and let the Holy Spirit lead you in all things.

PRAYER. *Mary, Mother of God, pray for me that I may be attentive to the Holy Spirit.*

AVE compassion for those who are wavering. —Jude 22

Compassion is key

REFLECTION. When Jesus finished telling the parable of the Good Samaritan He asked the lawyer a question: who was neighbor to the injured man? The answer came back: the one who acted with compassion.

At the end of each day, take some time to evaluate those moments when you showed compassion and those moments when you could have been more compassionate.

PRAYER. *Lord, may compassion mark every aspect of my day as I seek to serve others.*

 HE people of God want pastors, not clergy acting like bureaucrats or government officials. —Pope Francis

Priests are called to serve

REFLECTION. It may seem quite obvious that priests are called to serve yet there are some who use people and situations as stepping stones for their own advancement.

A true disciple of Jesus is not concerned with controlling the "purse strings" of a diocese or getting a "red hat." Pray for and encourage priests who model Jesus Christ in word and deed.

PRAYER. *Mary, be a mother to priests, especially to those who have forgotten their true vocation.*

BEING truly present and focused on the person right in front of you communicates love. —Dana Foley, R.N.

Eye to eye, heart to heart

REFLECTION. Practically every profession we can think of has an element of human contact and interaction. For those who serve, the danger can be in looking ahead to the next problem to be solved instead of being attentive to the person God has placed in front of you.

Consider each interaction you have as a moment to see the face of God in those He brings your way.

PRAYER. *Lord, reveal Your face in those whom I care for and serve.*

MY BRETHREN, consider it a cause of great joy whenever you endure various trials. —Jas 1:2

How do we view trials in life?

REFLECTION. Caregivers are on the front lines serving others when there is a crisis. Caregivers themselves, however, will go through trials just like everyone else. St. James tells us to consider it a joy when this happens. Either St. James is crazy or perhaps he is on to something.

Consider the trials you face as an opportunity to put your faith into practice and to trust God.

PRAYER. *Lord, while I fear trials, give me hope in the midst of them.*

LESSED is the man who perseveres when he is tempted. —Jas 1:12

We all face trials

REFLECTION. The Christian faith is not a sprint but rather a marathon. Throughout the four Gospels and the epistles in the New Testament, Christians are exhorted to endure. This means to continue on in faith even if we are unsure about the road we are taking.

Thank God that you are faithful in the midst of these temptations and are providing a beautiful example of what faith looks like.

PRAYER. *Jesus, save me from trials and grant me strength when temptations arise.*

VERYONE should be quick to listen but slow to speak and slow to anger. —Jas 1:19

Sound advice

REFLECTION. God gave us two ears and one mouth so we should use them in proportion to which He gave them. Perhaps in order to listen we should be asking good questions.

Good teachers have good answers, but great teachers ask great questions. Try asking good questions for it will show a profound respect to those you serve.

PRAYER. *Lord, may I spend time listening to You before I speak to others.*

OW happy I am to realize that I am little and weak; how happy I am to see myself so imperfect.

—St. Thérèse of Lisieux

Perfect imperfections

REFLECTION. St. Thérèse advocated for the "little way" of love. She promoted doing small things with great love. In a world which directs us to hide our imperfections, St. Thérèse was humble and gave all the credit to God.

We all have attributes as well as imperfections. Don't let the imperfections get you down, but offer all, even the imperfections, to God.

PRAYER. *Lord, be my strength in my imperfections; may I offer all my life to You.*

OR judgment will be without mercy to the one who has not shown mercy. — Jas 2:13

Be merciful

REFLECTION. The Hebrew word for mercy is *elios* which is the action of pouring out oil. In the same way, our understanding of mercy is not just an intellectual understanding of the word but a living out of the word.

It may be difficult to show mercy if you've never received it. Thankfully, Christians proclaim that the mercy of God is poured out on all. Receive His mercy and give it to others.

PRAYER. *Jesus, help me to receive Your mercy and to generously give it to others.*

ILENCE is key in discerning your calling in life. —Fran Manicotti

The gift or peace and quiet

REFLECTION. Those who serve others are usually A-type personalities who like to be in charge and like to get things done. We need them for they tend to be natural leaders.

It's important for these A-types to make time for some silence and reflection. Without silence, our lives will lack direction, and we may tend to listen to ourselves instead of God who wishes to quietly direct us.

PRAYER. *Lord God, may I value moments of silence in order to hear Your voice in my life.*

HY am I pursuing nursing? I witnessed how nurses took care of my father when he was sick. —Joyce Meadows, Student

The power of witness

REFLECTION. It's interesting to hear why people choose a career. I find that people often choose a career based on their positive experience with someone in the field. The same seems true for those who enter religious life.

Are there people who might point to you as someone who has been a witness to them?

PRAYER. *Jesus, thank You for being a positive example and inspiring me to be all You call me to be.*

NE "Thank you" can mean the difference between a great day and a routine day.

—Edward Kramden, Maintenance man

Words matter

REFLECTION. One of the greatest impacts we
can make doesn't cost a cent. Our words can
truly be the difference between someone having a great day or that same person feeling
unappreciated.

People of faith know that God sees and
appreciates our good works, but it's nice to hear
those words. Make time today to show appreciation to someone who works behind the scenes.

PRAYER. *St. Joseph, pray for me that I may be
a person who encourages and affirms others.*

OLERANCE is the virtue of the man
without convictions. —G.K. Chesterton

Be bold like Jesus

REFLECTION. It seems that the word and con-
cept of tolerance has become a "buzzword" in
schools and society. We are not to judge others
of course, but at the altar of tolerance do we
accept unacceptable behavior?

Jesus was not tolerant of people who looked
down on others or perverted God's law. Be bold
like Jesus and don't tolerate unacceptable
behavior. Be a person of justice.

PRAYER. *Jesus, grant me the wisdom and the
courage to speak up for justice's sake.*

IN THE same way, faith by itself is dead if it does not have works. —Jas 2:17

A lively faith in action

REFLECTION. St. James makes the statement that faith without deeds is dead. What then is faith? Is it just an intellectual assent to certain truths? For the Christian, faith must be put into action.

Think of how many opportunities you have each day to put your faith into action. Have faith in God's care for each and every person. Have faith that God has a plan for you which you live out in caring for others.

PRAYER. *Lord, may the truths that I learned about Catholicism be lived out each day.*

HIS faith was brought to completion by works. —Jas 2:22

Faith and works go hand in hand

REFLECTION. We express our faith in people and objects every day. When we press the light switch we have faith that the light will go on. When we go through a green light we have faith that others going in the other direction will stop.

Religious faith trusts both God and His word. Never be afraid to act on the faith God has revealed through His Church and in His word.

PRAYER. *Jesus, Word of God, guide me in my daily decisions both great and small.*

OU can see, then, that a man is justi-
fied by works and not by faith alone.

—Jas 2:24

APR. 4

Express your faith with joy

REFLECTION. How often do people compartmentalize their faith, thinking that it is only a
Sunday obligation? Our faith should be like a
thread that is woven through everything we
do. Our family life, social life, and job should
be positively impacted by what we believe.

Think of all the people you impact positively
because of your faith. You do make a difference!

PRAYER. *Lord, may all my works reflect my
belief in Your steadfast love and care.*

 OR just as the body is dead without a
spirit, so faith without works is also dead.

—Jas 2:26

APR. 5

Receive the Holy Spirit

REFLECTION. Catholics receive the Holy Spirit
during the reception of the sacrament of
Confirmation. Many of us were very young at
the time and perhaps didn't fully appreciate
what God was doing for and in us.

The same Spirit that enabled Jesus to respond
in love, mercy, and forgiveness is offered to us.
Take some time to ask the Holy Spirit to empower you for the work God has called you to.

PRAYER. *Come Holy Spirit, stir within my
heart to empower me to be like Jesus.*

I N THIS life we cannot do great things, only small things with great love.

—Mother Teresa

APR.

6

Start where you can

REFLECTION. This quote by Mother Teresa is an encouragement for so many people who wish to put their faith into action. We can begin by starting where God has placed us.

Do we live with others? Serve them in small ways. Do we know someone who lives alone? Visit them. Care for those you work with. Opportunities abound!

PRAYER. *Lord, open my eyes and heart to see You in those I live and work with.*

A LL the darkness in the world cannot extinguish the light of a single candle.

—St. Francis

APR.

7

Be the light

REFLECTION. How often do we feel that our work is insignificant or our efforts go unappreciated? The truth is that the work we do will not always be appreciated, yet it is significant!

St. Francis offers caregivers a ray of hope. Continue to be the light no matter how unappreciated your good work may be.

PRAYER. *Jesus, Light of the world, may I reflect the light that emanates from You.*

ONSIDER how a small fire can set ablaze a great forest. —Jas 3:5

APR. 8

Words have power

REFLECTION. St. James makes a comparison between the power of a raging fire and the words of our mouth. Words have been used to build people up and to tear them down. Words have broken friendships and reconciled enemies.

What a gift it is to use our words for the benefit and encouragement of others. Be generous with your praise.

PRAYER. *Lord, may my words be truthful and compassionate, seeking to build others up.*

 LITTLE bit of mercy makes the world less cold and more just.
—Pope Francis

APR. 9

Mercy, mercy, and mercy

REFLECTION. So important is mercy that Jesus includes it in His list of the Beatitudes when He says, "Blessed are the merciful." What does mercy look like? We can list some attributes of mercy, but mercy is best defined by the actions of people.

Jesus, first and foremost, embodies mercy, but so do you in the manner in which you care and serve others.

PRAYER. *Lord, may my words and actions be synonymous with mercy.*

OUT of the same mouth flow blessings and curses. This should not be so my brethren. —Jas 3:10

APR. 10

Be consistent in speech

REFLECTION. Catholics and all who call Jesus Lord are to be both salt and light in the world. It is a challenge to be both in many workplaces where the language can be uncharitable to say the least.

How can you make a difference? Give up the cursing, give up the negativity, and let your words flow from a heart that is full of the love of God.

PRAYER. *Mary, Mother of God, may my words be gentle, directing all to Jesus.*

IF CHRISTIANITY was something we were making up, of course we could make it easier. But it is not. —C. S. Lewis

APR. 11

Faith is not a joyride

REFLECTION. Critics of Christianity have tried to poke holes in many aspects of our faith over the centuries, yet Christianity remains.

If our origins were manmade then we would expect it to be quite easy to follow, but this is not the case. It's difficult because of our sin and attachments to things of this world. Is it easy? No. Rewarding? Yes!

PRAYER. *Lord, give me strength to overcome my sin through Your mercy and Holy Spirit.*

RAW near to God, and he will draw near to you. —Jas 4:8

APR.
12

He is waiting for you

REFLECTION. Faithful Catholics know well that Jesus is always present to us through prayer, His word, community, and sacraments. It's easy for us to draw near when we know how.

Consider others who don't have the benefit of faith as we do. How can you assist others in drawing near to God so that they may know of His love firsthand?

PRAYER. *Loving Lord, remind me that my faith is to be shared with others.*

 NYONE who knows the right thing to do and fails to do it commits a sin. —Jas 4:17

APR.
13

Knowledge of the truth matters

REFLECTION. The *Catechism of the Catholic Church* contains the teaching of the Church and is rooted in Scripture and sacred tradition. It's important to become familiar with what the Church teaches so we will not be in error and will be guided in the right way to live.

Have you grown up in the faith or have you grown old in the faith? Never stop growing!

PRAYER. *God, our Father, may You give me a hunger for Your word and for truth.*

COMMIT yourself to learning about the Catholic faith and share your understanding with others.

APR.
14

—St. Bernadette

Your spiritual growth benefits others

REFLECTION. It's always interesting to hear the stories of those who convert to the Catholic faith. They almost always speak of their misconceptions of what Catholics believe until they took a look for themselves.

As you grow in your faith and learn more, you will find that your knowledge and joy will be a great benefit to others.

PRAYER. *Lord, may my knowledge of the faith grow so I may share Your love with others.*

SERVICE as a firefighter means being ready to serve 24 hours a day.

APR.
15

—John J. Fagan

Always alert

REFLECTION. Firefighters are called for all sorts of emergencies. While we typically think of fighting fires as their number one job, it constitutes only a part of the job. When they are called to serve it's usually when something has gone tragically wrong.

Is our service to others compartmentalized or are we ready to serve others on their timetable?

PRAYER. *Jesus, give me the strength to serve and care for others no matter when.*

YOU too must be patient. Take courage, for the coming of the Lord is near.
—Jas 5:8

Just a little patience

REFLECTION. The word patience was once translated as the word "longsuffering."

I feel "longsuffering" more accurately describes what people go through while waiting for God to act. God is still in control and sovereign over all situations so let us take the advice of St. James and be patient for God is in control.

PRAYER. *Sovereign Lord, comfort me and others who wait patiently for You to act.*

INDEED, those who had perseverance are the ones we called blessed. —Jas 5:11

Learn from the Saints of old

REFLECTION. One of the gifts of being part of the Christian community is that we can look back and admire the faith of biblical characters and the Saints.

One common element that they exhibited was that they persevered through trials. Think of Abraham, Moses, Ruth, Esther, Jesus, the Apostles and many others who persevered. You are called to persevere as well.

PRAYER. *Lord, help me persevere when I don't see the end of the road in front of me.*

S ANYONE among you suffering? He should pray.
—Jas 5:13

Who is St. James speaking to?

REFLECTION. The most powerful words in evangelization are these: "May I pray with you?" Are you with someone who is suffering? Maybe a co-worker, a fellow teacher, or someone who is physically injured. Have you ever asked if you can pray for them or with them?

Don't wait for others; seize the opportunity and ask. Prayer changes lives!

PRAYER. *Lord, use me this day to pray for and with someone who needs prayer.*

 ERVING through AA has been the most humbling and life-affirming thing I've ever done.
—Gloria Manning

The first step

REFLECTION. Addictions and addictive behavior affect so many people that it's almost an epidemic. Each person who is addicted impacts family members, friends, co-workers, and the list goes on.

Thank God that many do seek help and can find a healthy way to manage their disease and behavior. Pray for those who care for people who are addicted.

PRAYER. *Jesus, may I be sensitive to those who are struggling with addictions.*

THE prayer of a righteous man is powerful and effective. —Jas 5:16

APR.
20

Be confident in your prayer

REFLECTION. To be righteous is to be in a good relationship with another. Men and women who are faithful to God have great power before the throne of God through prayer.

Let your requests be known to God each day. Spiritually speaking it's the best way we can serve each other. Pray with faith and intention. Thank God in advance for His response.

PRAYER. *Lord, may my voice rise to You each day in prayer.*

———————

THE light shines in the darkness, and the darkness has been unable to overcome it. —Jn 1:5

APR.
21

Light always wins

REFLECTION. Light and darkness are themes that run throughout the Gospel of St. John. Jesus will be revealed as the true light of the world as the story unfolds.

The darkness seems to get the upper hand when Jesus is nailed to the Cross, however. Jesus is humiliated, beaten, and killed. In the end, Jesus is raised from the dead and thus defeated even the darkness of death.

PRAYER. *Jesus, be my light in times of darkness and confusion so I may never lose hope.*

OPE = Help One Person Every day.
—John Moore

Plain and simple

REFLECTION. No matter where you are or what position you have you can always make a positive difference. Jesus often interacted with one person at a time. Consider Jesus speaking to Nicodemus, the Samaritan woman at the well, the sick man at the pool of Bethesda, and many more.

Who will you help today? Who has reached out and helped you?

PRAYER. *Lord, never let me discount the value of helping one person at a time.*

ERVING as a mother is life's greatest blessing and brings an unconditional love that never dies.
—Colleen O'Donnell Thorburn

APR.
23

From the moment of conception

REFLECTION. A mother's love is like no other. When her child suffers she suffers all the more. When her child takes their first steps she is there to catch them if they fall, and this will continue throughout the child's life well into adulthood.

Yet, it is the mother who sees this as a great blessing, and there we get a window into the love of God who loves us with a mother's love.

PRAYER. *Jesus, pray for mothers as they reflect God's unconditional love.*

63

HE Rosary is the "weapon" for these times.
—St. Padre Pio

APR. 24

Life can be a battle

REFLECTION. Some people have difficulty with using military imagery and terminology when discussing spirituality. When we consider that Jesus Himself used military imagery perhaps it gives us a moment to ponder what we are involved in with the spiritual life.

We are in a spiritual battle and our "weapons" are prayer, the sacraments, and following the peaceful way of Christ.

PRAYER. *Mary, may I reflect on the life of Jesus in order to draw strength to serve others.*

ACH one of them is Jesus in disguise.
—Mother Teresa

APR. 25

Looking with the eyes of faith

REFLECTION. Mother Teresa is a Saint yet she was born of flesh and blood just like you and me. What then is the difference between those recognized as Saints and ordinary Catholics?

Perhaps it's just the way we view others through the lens of faith. Do we view others as problems, sinners, or by their faults, or do we see Jesus disguised in their humanity?

PRAYER. *Lord Jesus, forgive me for those times I failed to recognize You and serve You in my neighbor.*

ACCORDING to Scripture, it is the heart that prays.

—St. Joseph Guide to the Catechism

Heart to heart

REFLECTION. What comes from the heart touches the heart. How true this is when it comes to prayer.

Traditional prayers are of great value and have been a source of comfort to others down through the ages, but the prayer of the heart is the most pure. Use traditional prayers but also speak to God from your heart and it will touch the heart of God.

PRAYER. *Jesus, I love You and desire only to do Your will. Help guide me.*

IT'S for you Jesus, if you want it, I want it too.

—Blessed Chiara Badano

A beautiful role model

REFLECTION. Blessed Chiara died of cancer in 1990 at the tender age of eighteen. Her spiritual life was mature—well beyond her young life.

It's easy to praise God when things are going well but when adversity befalls us then our faith is tested. Whatever God does, He does beautifully and perfectly, even when we may not know what He's doing.

PRAYER. *My Lord and God, I trust in Your love for me in good times and in bad.*

LOVE for the children is the best instructor in their upbringing. Only to the one who loves children may they be entrusted.

—Blessed Pauline Von Mallinckrodt

APR.
28

Love comes first

REFLECTION. For those who care and serve others love is a prerequisite. You can have all the training in the world but without love your work will just be a job and not a vocation.

Not every day will be easy and some people are more lovable than others, yet the fact remains that having a passion and love for people will always make the good teacher better.

PRAYER. *Lord, may I serve others with love, knowing that I serve You in them.*

HE HIMSELF was not the light; his role was to bear witness to the light.

—Jn 1:8

APR.
29

Point the way for others

REFLECTION. John the Baptist had a very specific role in the Gospel. His role was to point others to Jesus.

This is in fact the role of every disciple. We can point others to Jesus through our words and actions so that they, too, can enter into a relationship with Christ. Thank you for serving and caring for others: you too are a light pointing to Jesus.

PRAYER. *St. John the Baptist, pray for me that I may lead others to God.*

E CAME to his own, but his own did not accept him. —Jn 1:11

Not everyone will acknowledge your service

REFLECTION. One of the difficult parts of caring for others and serving is that no matter how good a job you do and no matter how much you try there always seem to be people who don't appreciate you.

Maybe there is some solace in the fact that Jesus was rejected too. Continue to do good, be good, and be a power for good.

PRAYER. *Jesus, may my focus be on doing the right thing and not on what others may think.*

ND the word became flesh and dwelt among us. —Jn 1:14

How do you dwell with others?

REFLECTION. Jesus left His throne in Heaven and through the Blessed Virgin Mary became man. How humbling must it have been for God to become man and dwell amongst us.

Jesus did not thumb His nose at humanity but rather embraced them and loved them. How do you dwell with others? Ask God for the grace to be humble.

PRAYER. *Lord God, make me humble like You in all my dealings with others.*

HAT are you looking for?
—Jn 1:38

Great teachers ask exceptional questions

REFLECTION. Good teachers have good answers but great teachers ask exceptional questions. It can be easily argued that there has been no greater teacher than Jesus. The first words out of Jesus' mouth are a question.

Take some quiet time and reflect on this question and see where the answer will take you.

PRAYER. *Jesus, Teacher, may I reflect on Your questions in order to find my purpose.*

Y DAD spent his life dedicated to service through sharing his time with helping children through music for over 20 years.

—Debra DeLeon, Daughter

A dad's good example

REFLECTION. Some of our actions have ripple effects that we may never fully realize in this life. While we may want to influence others through our actions, how significant are those acts of caring and service in the eyes of our children over whom we have the biggest influence?

What will your family remember about you? What ripple effects will be passed on through your children?

PRAYER. *St. Cecilia, patroness of musicians, may my life be a song offered to God.*

I MEET people when they most need support and kindness. It is very gratifying to offer help.
—Ellen Brandt, EMT

MAY 4

In times of crisis

REFLECTION. Our family has a tradition of praying when we see an ambulance racing by. We pray for the victims but also for those who will be first on the scene during the critical moments when life and death hang in the balance.

Take some time to pray for and thank those who are on the front lines of service when they meet people who need support and kindness.

PRAYER. *Lord God, assist those who care through healing others as You did.*

"CAN anything good come from Nazareth?" Philip replied, "Come and see."
—Jn 1:46

MAY 5

Where is the good?

REFLECTION. Many times we can make judgments without knowing all of the facts. We may hear that a person has such and such a job or lives in this particular city and we make a judgment.

The early disciples were in the same boat for Nazareth didn't have a noble reputation. Yet the words of Philip challenge us today: "Come and see." Take time to re-evaluate previous judgments.

PRAYER. *Lord, may my view of others not be tainted by my sin and false judgments.*

DO WHATEVER he tells you. — Jn 2:5 **MAY 6**

Mary's last recorded words

REFLECTION. Mary, the Mother of God, says very little in the pages of the New Testament. Her last words, however, are powerful indeed. Mary points the way to Jesus. We honor Mary best when we do what her Son asks.

Those who serve and care for others are on the top of the list of those who do respond to the words and person of Jesus. Like Mary, point to Jesus in all you do.

PRAYER. *Hail Mary, full of grace, pray for me that I may do what Jesus asks of me.*

NO ONE can see the kingdom of God without being born from above.
—Jn 3:3 **MAY 7**

An ongoing process of rebirth

REFLECTION. Being born is a one-time event. Being born again spiritually is an ongoing event in which we continually go deeper.

When caring for others we will at times be forced to grow spiritually because of what life throws at us. Those times of growth can be difficult, but like a snake that sheds its skin, it is necessary in order to grow.

PRAYER. *Lord, may You lead me in my spiritual growth and may I embrace any changes.*

LOOK for the best qualities in my students and work to promote, guide, and nourish those. —Ellen Brandt, Teacher

MAY 8

The classroom of life

REFLECTION. Hopefully we can reflect on that one teacher who saw something in us, who even challenged us and got on our case because they knew we could do better.

Teaching and learning doesn't end in the classroom obviously. Your care and modeling Christ-like behavior is the best teacher of faith. See the best in others.

PRAYER. *Jesus, help me to teach as You taught and challenged others to be all they could be.*

 OR God did not send his son into the world to condemn the world but in order that the world may be saved through him. —Jn 3:17

MAY 9

The heart of God the Father

REFLECTION. The heart of God the Father is most often seen in the heart of those who serve and care for others. Take solace in the fact that when you reach out to those on the margins you are reflecting the same love that God has for us.

It can be tempting to condemn when behavior is bad, but look for ways to care in the midst of it.

PRAYER. *Lord, help me to reach out in love rather than condemnation.*

E MUST increase; I must decrease.
—Jn 3:30

MAY
10

The life of every disciple

REFLECTION. The final words of St. John the Baptist reflect or should reflect the words of every disciple. The Greek word for "I" is "ego." As a follower of Jesus it is not our will that is important but God's will.

Caregivers reveal this attribute whenever they put the needs of others before themselves. Thank you for being an agent of God's grace and for allowing God's grace to increase in you.

PRAYER. *Lord, help me die to myself in order that You may increase in me.*

MUST remember my job as stepparent is to provide support not only to my step child, but to his parents. —Ellen Brandt, Stepmother

MAY
11

Stepparent heroes!

REFLECTION. Being a parent is difficult work. Being a stepparent is perhaps more difficult because there are added challenges and relationships to negotiate. The selfless love of a stepparent recognizes that they must support the child's parents which must involve dying to self.

Pray for stepparents that they may seek the benefit of the child and support the parents.

PRAYER. *St. Joseph, pray for stepparents to be faithful in their roles.*

E WHO God meant you to be and you will set the world on fire.

—St. Catherine of Siena

MAY 12

The courage to be silent and listen

REFLECTION. St. Catherine of Siena was an ardent follower of Jesus and a fierce defender of the faith even reprimanding a pope who was going astray. So, who has God called you to be?

This question can't be answered for you by others but is revealed only in the silence of your own heart. Take some time to listen to and discern God's will for you.

PRAYER. *Lord, help me be the person who You created me to be.*

NTICIPATE the needs of others and they will never forget your act of kindness. —John Lydon, Physical Therapist

MAY 13

Look ahead and act

REFLECTION. It can be hard enough to take care of our needs and that of our family, let alone the needs of others. Think of those people who have anticipated your needs.

Recall actions from your parents and friends who you would like to serve or honor. Start with one person a month and you will make a huge difference.

PRAYER. *Lord God, may my caring and service for others reflect Your love for me as You anticipate my needs.*

HE HAD to pass through Samaria.
—Jn 4:4

The things we have to do

REFLECTION. The Gospel tells us that Jesus had to pass through Samaria. It was a Divine imperative, it was God's will for Him. Think of all the things you have to do each day that may be routine and even monotonous.

Jesus found a way to turn a chance meeting into a life-changing event. Look for ways to turn the ordinary into the extraordinary.

PRAYER. *Merciful God, help me recognize Your will in the ordinary things of life.*

THE water I will give him will become a spring of water within him welling up to eternal life.
—Jn 4:14

A spring for others

REFLECTION. The woman who Jesus spoke to at the well in Samaria was only interested in life-giving water for herself at first. She seemingly failed to hear Jesus' words that she was to be a "spring for others."

The gift of faith that we have received is not for us alone. We are to be a spring for others, a resource that overflows because the source of our life is God Himself. Continue to overflow!

PRAYER. *Jesus, fill me with Your Holy Spirit that I may serve those with the same Spirit You had.*

ESUS told her, "Go, call your husband and then come back here." —Jn 4:16

Go, call, come back

REFLECTION. When we've encountered Jesus there will be a mission that follows. We may not believe that God wants to use us but it's true.

Jesus called a sinful Samaritan woman to be a witness to her community two thousand years ago. She may have thought her witness would be ignored, but Jesus had faith in her. Jesus has that same faith in you to go and make a difference.

PRAYER. *My Lord and God, thank You for Your faith in me to be part of Your mission on earth.*

Y YOURSELF you will do nothing, but if you have God as the center of all your action, then you will reach the goal.
—Bl. Pier Giorgio Frassati

God alone is enough

REFLECTION. Blessed Pier Frassati lived a short life but a meaningful one. An athletic and faithful young man who loved sports and the outdoors, he put Jesus first in all things. He was a passionate social justice advocate, he gathered his friends to help serve and care for the marginalized, sick, and less fortunate.

His focus was on Jesus and the rest fell into place. What is your passion?

PRAYER. *Blessed Pier, may your example be an inspiration to me, and may I inspire others.*

THE man believed what Jesus said to him, and he departed. —Jn 4:50

Faith leads the way

REFLECTION. Throughout the Gospels people respond various ways to Jesus. Some believe, some are doubtful, and a few are even hostile to Jesus and His message. What is your response?

At times we may doubt and even have some hostility to Jesus' call to love even our enemies. Walk by faith trusting in Jesus' unconditional love for you and you will be at peace.

PRAYER. *Holy Spirit, lead me in the way of Jesus, trusting in His word and empowered by the Spirit.*

O YOU want to get well? —Jn 5:6

An obvious answer one would think

REFLECTION. Jesus asks a man who has been ill for thirty-eight years a curious question: "Do you want to be well?" The obvious answer would be a resounding "Yes."

This man speaks about his inability to get to the "healing" water. Jesus takes the initiative and reaches out and heals him. Jesus has the desire and ability to heal all ills.

PRAYER. *Lord, may my focus be on You as I reach out and offer care to others.*

T IS I. Do not be afraid! —Jn 6:20 **MAY**

20

What gives us courage?

REFLECTION. The disciples were afraid. Out in the middle of the Sea of Galilee they see what they think is a ghost. Jesus speaks, "It is I. Do not be afraid!" What gives the disciples peace is the presence of Jesus.

That same Jesus is present to you and me. He is present in His word and in the sacraments. Turn to Him; He desires to give you peace.

PRAYER. *Lord, I am often afraid of the future and what it may hold. Be with me.*

HE pressure that one wrong decision can gravely affect another life can be overwhelming. —Ellen Brandt, EMT **MAY**

21

We act in faith

REFLECTION. Often we have time to ponder and discern our next plan of action. Those who serve in emergency medical situations don't have that luxury. Preparation precedes their actions, but every now and again they are confronted with a unique situation.

Pray for those who serve people during extremely stressful and life-threatening situations that they have the wisdom to do what is needed.

PRAYER. *Lord, be with EMT's as they respond to people in emergency situations.*

ESUS answered them, "I am the bread of life."

—Jn 6:35

MAY 22

Who sustains your faith?

REFLECTION. In one of the most shocking statements in the New Testament Jesus proclaims Himself the "bread of life." Catholics have celebrated the Eucharist at the command of Jesus.

In this sacrament we receive Jesus, body, blood, soul, and divinity. Caregivers need to have a source from which to draw strength to care for others. Jesus awaits in the Eucharist.

PRAYER. *Jesus, may I receive You reverently in the Eucharist to sustain me through my trials.*

HE words I have spoken to you are spirit and life.

—Jn 6:63

MAY 23

What is contained in your words?

REFLECTION. Spending time reading the Scriptures is vital to maintain a healthy spiritual life. Reflecting on the words of Jesus can comfort and challenge us.

This should give us pause to reflect on our own words. Are the words we speak vehicles for comfort? Can we challenge people to put their faith into practice?

PRAYER. *Jesus, Word of God, may my words provide hope and comfort to those I care for.*

E MUST speak to them with our hands by giving, before we try to speak to them with our lips.

—St. Peter Claver

MAY
24

What do our actions communicate?

REFLECTION. St. Peter Claver spent much of his life tending to the needs of those who were coming off the slave ships.

Think of the countless acts of mercy you have performed with your hands. Hands that have served food, hugged loved ones, and been placed together to pray. The best witness you may have given was without words.

PRAYER. *Holy Spirit, my Advocate, empower me to move forward imitating Jesus my Lord.*

O ACT of caring is little or insignificant, it has ripple effects that we may never see.

—J.J. Marshal, Funeral Home Director

MAY
25

Attention to details

REFLECTION. We count on the skill and diligence of those who take care of us when we come into this world, and we expect the same of those who are present at the end of our lives.

Funeral home professionals know that when they meet most of their clients they are to some degree sad and grieving. Little acts of kindness matter at the beginning, end, and all throughout life.

PRAYER. *Jesus, this is the day You have made, may I do my best to make it a good day.*

FTER this, many of his disciples turned away and no longer remained with him.
—Jn 6:66

Did they really turn away from Jesus?

REFLECTION. Most faithful Catholics, treasure the words of Jesus and can't imagine turning away from Him. Yet, people did. If some people rejected Jesus then it follows that some will reject us too.

Take courage! We care and serve not because of what others believe but because of what we believe. Continue being a light and shine.

PRAYER. *Jesus, Light of the world, shine in me when times are dark and we need Your light.*

UST holding a hand and offering comfort can turn a difficult moment around.
—Ellen Bryant, EMT

Small things, great love

REFLECTION. Most of the people EMT's and emergency workers encounter are strangers. Many quickly become friends due to the amount of care and comfort they receive during a difficult moment.

Whether you are called on to minister to a friend or a stranger doesn't matter, they are equally loved by God.

PRAYER. *Gracious God, thank You for the grace to reach out to all those who suffer.*

I T WAS a great "soul" move, not a financial move. —Dr. O'Connell, Doctor to the Homeless

Taking it to the streets

REFLECTION. Dr. O'Connell traded in a residency as an oncologist for a life of treating the homeless in Boston. His office is the street. His patients have neither money nor housing. He offers them his care and service free of charge. He is Christ-like.

How can you use your gifts and talents to benefit those who have no way of repaying you?

PRAYER. *Lord, help me to use the gifts You gave me to serve those on the margins.*

S TOP judging by appearances, but judge justly. —Jn 7:24

They are Jesus in disguise

REFLECTION. Jesus says plainly that it's easy to love those who love you. The difficult thing is to love those who by all outward appearances are unlovable. Let's face it, there are people who will resist any care you may offer. The temptation is to dismiss them.

To judge justly is to see them through the eyes of God, through the lens of faith. Care for them as you would care for Jesus.

PRAYER. *Lord, You know that the struggle to love and offer care is real. Help me to be patient.*

GOOD sense of humor is vital in teaching the little ones.
—Sr. Mary Elizabeth, S.C.C.

MAY 30

A sense of humor is a sign of the Spirit

REFLECTION. In the same way an engine needs oil to help keep it moving, a healthy sense of humor is the oil that keeps us going through life and is absolutely necessary for caregivers.

Seeing the humor in situations can keep you sane. Remember, Jesus must have had a good sense of humor, and we are created in His image.

PRAYER. *Lord, may I not take myself so seriously that I fail to see Your hand in my life.*

 E CRY out only when there is hope that someone may hear us.
—Jean Vanier

MAY 31

Notice people's silence

REFLECTION. Jean Vanier has spent his life working with the marginalized and disenfranchised. Visiting a home for abandoned children he noticed the squalor in which they were living.

He then noticed the silence. There was a room full of children yet no crying because there was no one to hear them. Notice the silence of others as a call for help.

PRAYER. *Jesus, may my ears and eyes be attuned to the cries and silence of others.*

DO YOUR best. Start where you can. **JUNE**
One step at a time.

1

—Charlie Kramden, Counselor

We can all do something

REFLECTION. Sometimes we feel overwhelmed, unprepared, and at times isolated. Although all these things may be true, life still moves forward. What are we to do?

One option is to collapse and spiral downward into despair. The other is to take one small step forward and then another. If you're not overwhelmed, help someone who is.

PRAYER. *Jesus, give me strength to carry on and the wisdom to help others who struggle.*

CARING means always doing the right **JUNE**
thing in a positive manner even in a dangerous and negative environment.

2

—Sgt. Gerry Doran, Corrections Officer

Serve and protect all

REFLECTION. Jesus remarked that there is not much glory in loving those who love you back. The true measure is caring for those who don't love you or may have committed a heinous crime.

While we may not "feel" love towards criminals perhaps the best we can do is to be positive, non-judgmental, and kind. You may be the only one in their life who cares.

PRAYER. *Jesus, may Your joy and peace fill me when I am called to serve in a difficult situation.*

I AM not afraid. I was born to do this.

—St. Joan of Arc

JUNE 3

Born to run

REFLECTION. When St. Joan was asked if she knew she was in God's grace, she answered: "If I am not, may God put me there; and if I am, may God so keep me."

We all have work to do which involves caring for others. Some will directly serve the needs of others while others serve indirectly. Whatever the case, stay in God's grace and follow His will in your life day and night.

PRAYER. *Lord Jesus, keep me in God's grace, and when I stray bring me back.*

JESUS Christ is counting on you! The Church is counting on you! The pope is counting on you! —Pope Francis

JUNE 4

No pressure here!

REFLECTION. Pope Francis makes a bold statement which can seemingly put a lot of pressure on us. Jesus, the Church, and the Pope are all counting on me! Yikes! That's quite a load to carry!

What is Pope Francis counting on? He's counting on us to follow the call of Jesus and be true to our baptismal call. We live this out by serving one another. Yes, we are counting on you.

PRAYER. *Mary, as you followed God's will for you, pray that I may follow God's will for me.*

PARENTS are the primary educators of the faith. **JUNE** **5**
—*Familiaris Consortio*

Teach by example

REFLECTION. I once gave a talk to senior citizens, most of whom were children in the 1920s and '30s. When the topic of how faith was lived in the home they could all recall moments where faith was lived out, and spoke about these events as if they happened yesterday.

It wasn't what their parents said that made an impact so many years later, but rather, how they acted because of the faith they had.

PRAYER. *Lord, may I be a living witness to Your love and provide a good example to all.*

CARING means doing a job well that few understand and even fewer appreciate. **JUNE** **6**
—Sgt. Gerry Doran, Corrections Officer

Even when the spotlight isn't on you

REFLECTION. There are many jobs that we would never want to do, but we are thankful that someone is doing them. Correction officers make an incredible contribution each day to both the protection of society and the potential rehabilitation of those inside.

Most of us will never enter the facilities they work in, but we are nevertheless comforted by knowing that they are present doing their job.

PRAYER. *Lord, protect those who work in difficult and dangerous circumstances.*

85

ET anyone among you who is without sin be the first to throw a stone at her.
—Jn 8:7

Release the grip on your stone

REFLECTION. It can feel good to say, "I told you so," and we can get some satisfaction in casting our harsh words at others. While we may no longer throw stones, we have ways of using words and actions to look down upon others.

The words of Jesus should cause us to release our grip on any unkind words and actions. Use this energy to seek positive ways to improve the way we serve others.

PRAYER. *Lord, give me the grace to forgive and the fortitude to let go of my condemnation of others.*

_____

 AM the light of the world. The one who follows me will never walk in darkness.
—Jn 8:12

Walk in the light

REFLECTION. Jesus is not only the light of the world but we, His disciples, are also called to be the light of the world.

Our light emanates from our relationship with Jesus so we must make sure that we are connected to Him through His word, prayer, and the sacraments. As a caregiver, you reflect His light.

PRAYER. *Jesus, may my actions reveal Your love to those I will meet today.*

F YOU remain faithful to my word, you will truly be my disciples.　　—Jn 8:31

JUNE
9

Close to the Sacred Heart

REFLECTION. Jesus uses the word "remain" several times throughout the Gospel of St. John. This word is sometimes translated as "abide." Jesus uses it in reference to the Eucharist and His word.

The temptation of course is to not remain, to flee, or just forget Jesus and His word. Make time for Jesus, present both in the Eucharist and in His word, and you will truly be His disciple.

PRAYER. *St John, increase my love for Jesus and for His word.*

OU forgive others all the time so feel free to forgive yourself.
　　—Jane Meadows, Counselor

JUNE
10

You can set yourself free

REFLECTION. I have found that most people have an easier time forgiving others than they do themselves. Caregivers desire to do the right thing, provide help at the right time, and be present when there is a need. The truth is that perfection comes only in Heaven.

True humility recognizes that we are loved despite our imperfections. Forgive yourself and allow God's forgiveness to define you.

PRAYER. *Jesus, overwhelm me with Your forgiveness and help me to move forward in life.*

GOD still has a dwelling place for us in Heaven even if we reject it.
—Frank O'Shea, Teacher

The agony of the separation

REFLECTION. The idea that God does not destroy what He has prepared for us leaves us with the thought that God not only loves us but "aches" for us. The dwelling place God has prepared is a reminder to Him of a relationship not realized.

We experience that same "ache" when our love or service is rejected. Stay close to God and let others know of God's "ache" for them.

PRAYER. *St. Thérèse, may the small things I do in love draw people to consider God.*

BUT one thing I do know: I was blind, and now I am able to see.
—Jn 9:25

Vision check

REFLECTION. It can be frustrating to be with someone who doesn't see things the same way as you do. Not that one is wrong and the other is right, sometimes it's just a matter of perspective.

Catholics have a way of viewing the world and others from another perspective than those who don't share our faith in Jesus. Through your loving service you can help others see the way Christ sees.

PRAYER. *St. Agnes, pray for me that my view may not be tainted by sin and selfishness.*

THE sheep follow him because they know his voice. —Jn 10:4

Whose voice do you listen to?

REFLECTION. Each and every day it seems we are bombarded with hundreds if not thousands of messages from the advertising world. They are all trying to persuade us to purchase something or convince us to vote one way or another.

God's voice is out there as well. Perhaps not on billboards or on television, but God continues to speak in the silence of the heart. Listen, He will lead you.

PRAYER. *Jesus, my shepherd, lead me and speak in such a way that I may hear You.*

AND I lay down my life for my sheep. —Jn 10:15

The actions of the Good Shepherd

REFLECTION. When a shepherd is out to pasture with his sheep he will often build a "pen" in order to corral them. He is thinking of the safety of the sheep. Good shepherds lay down where the gate would be.

This is a costly demonstration of love. He is the gate. In what ways have you been a good shepherd to those entrusted to you?

PRAYER. *Lord, may the care I receive from You be modeled in all of my behavior.*

WHEN my grandfather was in the hospital the nurse remembered all of our names.

JUNE 15

—Eva Gonzalez, Student

God knows us by our name

REFLECTION. The experience of a young student who encountered a caring nurse while her grandfather was ill, led her to pursue nursing. What a gift it is to have that level of caring that you make it a point to remember names.

We can give the excuse that, "I'm not good with names," or we can make the extra effort to form that bond of respect which begins with a name.

PRAYER. *My God, to think that You know my name! May I make the effort to know the names of others.*

AND the Father are one. —Jn 10:30

JUNE 16

One in being, one in heart

REFLECTION. While Jesus is the visible image of the invisible God, many of us have the experience of being very similar to our spouse or best friend. We are in sync with how they think and can anticipate their reactions.

When we are in union with Jesus, we too can know the Father's will—to love, forgive, serve, and care for one another. That is union with God.

PRAYER. *Lord, knowing Your will can be difficult. Help me to develop Your heart and mind.*

JESUS began to weep.   —Jn 11:35 **JUNE 17**

The humanity of Jesus is on display for all

REFLECTION. St. John's Gospel portrays Jesus as the exalted Word of God, the Light of the world, and the Resurrection and the Life. He also shows us the humanity of Jesus who is thirsty, tired, and one who weeps.

Caregivers will see people when they are most vulnerable. God has placed you here in this moment and this time to make a difference in the lives of those who are in need.

PRAYER. *Lord, may I recognize Your face in those who are most vulnerable.*

JESUS said, "Take away the stone."   —Jn 11:39 **JUNE 18**

Jesus asked for help

REFLECTION. In the miracle where Jesus raised Lazarus from the dead, Jesus asked for help. Sounds strange, doesn't it?

Before Lazarus came from darkness to light, from death to life, ordinary people helped move a stone in order that Lazarus could respond to the voice of God. What stones can you help move?

PRAYER. *Merciful God, help me remove stones of sorrow, suffering, and pain from the lives of others.*

SERVING through hospice has given me a new perspective on living and dying well. —Joan Steffan, R.N.

JUNE 19

God is always present

REFLECTION. At every stage of life God is present. We know this as Catholics, but we tend to question this when suffering is at hand. Even in the darkest hours God is there, calling us ever closer to Himself.

The atheist sees the darkness as proof that there is no God. Those who believe see it as an invitation to move forward in faith towards God.

PRAYER. *St. John of the Cross, help me to move forward through times of spiritual darkness.*

I HAVE four awesome grandparents named; Noni, Pepe, Grandma, and Grandpa. —Annalise DeLeon, Student

JUNE 20

The gift of grandparents

REFLECTION. Where do we find the gift of unconditional love? In God, yes! The second place that most people find unconditional love is in their grandparents. What a gift to have been loved by these awesome people.

Even when they are no longer with us we know that their love extends through eternity. Thank your grandparents and pray for them as they pray for you.

PRAYER. *St. Anne and St. Joachim, grandparents of Jesus, pray for us that we may love unconditionally.*

THE house was filled with the fragrance of the ointment. —Jn 12:3

**JUNE
21**

Be the fragrance!

REFLECTION. Smell is one of the most powerful memory generators that we possess. Various smells such as perfumes, the beach, and even cigars can remind us of the places and people associated with those smells.

We are called to be the fragrance of Christ. This means that through our caring and service we are to leave a lasting memory, one which will remind others of God's presence.

PRAYER. *Holy Spirit, stir within me to think, act, and speak like Jesus Christ, my Lord.*

IF ANYONE serves me, my Father will honor that person. —Jn 12:26

**JUNE
22**

Loved and honored by God

REFLECTION. In this brief passage Jesus links the two words of service and honor. This may come as second nature to Catholics, yet in antiquity honor was often accrued by force and dominance, not service.

How beautiful and humble are the words of Jesus. Service is what gets the attention of the Father. May your acts of service be honored by God as His loving son or daughter.

PRAYER. *Lord, knowing that You notice my small actions is all the reward I need.*

FTER Jesus had said this, he departed and hid himself from their sight.

—Jn 12:36

JUNE

23

Hide and seek with Christ

REFLECTION. At various times in the Gospels we read of Jesus retreating, removing Himself from the crowds. Isn't this true in our own lives as well? We can feel really close to Jesus one minute, and next we feel as if Jesus is hiding Himself from us.

Feelings are not the best indicator of how faithful we are. We know that while feelings may fade, Christ walks with us. Rely on faith, not feelings.

PRAYER. *Jesus, I accept those times when You are hidden from me. May I still be faithful.*

 E HAD loved his own who were in the world, and he loved them to the end.

—Jn 13:1

JUNE

24

Love through service

REFLECTION. The second half of St. John's Gospel is commonly referred to as the book of glory. How would you expect the book of glory to begin? With a miracle? With a dramatic display of power? The book of glory begins with Jesus washing His disciples' feet around a table.

Thank you for being a footwasher through your service to others. Your caring is love in action.

PRAYER. *Lord, thank You for caring for me. May my response be to care for others.*

DO NOT let your hearts be troubled.
—Jn 14:1

Who is your God?

REFLECTION. Perhaps Jesus speaks so often about worry and fear because He knows how troubled and fearful we can be. When our hearts are troubled who or what do we turn to?

Those who have faith, turn to Jesus. Through prayer, through reading His word, and through the sacraments we turn to our God who promises His presence through whatever storm we may be encountering.

PRAYER. *Lord, still the troubled waters of my heart so I may experience Your peace and love.*

WHOEVER loves me will keep my word.
—Jn 14:23

Trust the process

REFLECTION. Caregivers know that there is often a process to recovery. Nurses, doctors, and physician assistants have been trained to follow certain standards and procedures which will aid the healing process.

Catholics can rely on God's word and the two thousand year tradition of the Church. He is faithful. Trust His word.

PRAYER. *Jesus, the Word of God, I trust in You. Help me to be faithful to Your word.*

PEACE I leave with you, my peace I give to you.
—Jn 14:27

JUNE
27

Reconciled to God and others

REFLECTION. When we hear the word "peace," we can think of the absence of war or the sense of quiet and tranquility. These can all be true and in the biblical sense there is still another meaning. When Jesus says, "Go in peace," it means that the person is reconciled with God and also with a community.

The peace He gives does the same today. What do you leave behind? Let us be people of peace.

PRAYER. *Mary, Our Lady of Peace, pray that my life be one of reconciliation and joy.*

GET up! Let us be on our way.
—Jn 14:31

JUNE
28

Start where you can, start now

REFLECTION. Jesus knew that the road He was called to travel would not be easy. He took it anyway. Our road will also have bumps and dead-ends. We will not always know where it will lead.

Like Jesus, we need to be active participants in the life of faith and follow where the Lord calls us. We may not know where we are going, but we know who we are going with: Jesus Christ.

PRAYER. *Lord, the road can be rough, but I will follow You wherever You may lead.*

96

OD never tires of forgiving us; we are the ones who tire of seeking his mercy.
—Pope Francis

The Father's heart is filled with mercy

REFLECTION. There are times when we feel we are imposing on others. We may feel that we have overstepped our welcome or have asked too many favors. When it comes to God these feelings and perceptions can creep in as well.

Pope Francis reminds us that we can never exhaust the mercy of God. Seek His mercy often and show mercy, too.

PRAYER. *Merciful God, may I never tire of seeking Your mercy and sharing it.*

 F ALL human activities, man's listening to God is the supreme act of his reasoning and will. —Pope Paul VI

Beyond the "buzz"

REFLECTION. In modern advertising there is the ever-present quest to get your message above the "buzz"—to make your message or product stand out from the rest. God has a pretty good message as well. Yet, God tends to work through silence, and He speaks directly to the heart.

If we are always noisy and busy we may miss His calls. Take time for yourself and rest in silence.

PRAYER. *Lord, may Your word and Holy Spirit speak to my heart.*

WHENEVER we encounter another person in love, we learn something new about God.

— Pope Francis

JULY 1

Always be open to others

REFLECTION. There are people whom we will encounter who may not be pleasant, kind, or welcoming. As a person who cares for others we know this to be true. However, we don't love because others love us, we love because Christ loved us and calls us to do the same.

Take Pope Francis' advice and approach all with love; in doing so we will learn something about God.

PRAYER. *Lord, send Your Spirit to live, move, and love through me.*

I AM the vine, you are the branches. —Jn 15:5

JULY 2

Stay close to the True Vine

REFLECTION. The job of the branch is to stay close or to abide on the vine if it wishes to be fruitful. Jesus knew that this image would connect with his listeners for they were very familiar with vines and the making of wine.

Our work flows from our connection with Christ so we don't have to feel like we need to do a multitude of things. One thing is necessary.

PRAYER. *Heavenly Father, may I always be connected to You in good times and in bad.*

SOMETIMES a simple meal together at the diner makes all the difference.

—John Silk

Ah, the simple things in life

REFLECTION. Food brings people together and in some cultures food equals love. Perhaps you have a relative who is constantly seeking to feed you even after you're stuffed. It's a great gift to give and to receive.

Make time for the simple things in life and make time for your friends and family through sharing meals together. They will be the memories you most cherish.

PRAYER. *Jesus, You loved having meals with people. Help me to relax and enjoy the same.*

BY THIS is my Father glorified, that you bear much fruit and become my disciples.

—Jn 15:8

Be fruitful in word and deed

REFLECTION. The word fruit and the call to "fruitfulness" occurs many times in the Bible. St. Paul says that the fruit of the spirit is: love, joy, peace, patience, kindness, gentleness and self-control.

We become fruitful as a result of our abiding in Jesus, and it is His work through us that makes us fruitful. Examine how fruitful you have been this week.

PRAYER. *Lord, may I always give You credit for Your Holy Spirit working in and through me.*

EMAIN in my love. —Jn 15:9 **JULY 5**

Stay forever

REFLECTION. Jesus desires our love. That's pretty much the return that we can give Him back for all that He has done for us. Jesus will go on to say that we "remain" in His love by keeping His word.

We can certainly read and even memorize His word, and we can keep His word by living it out. Whenever you serve, care, forgive, and pray you remain in His love.

PRAYER. *Lord, help me to remain in Your love which overflows from Your Sacred Heart.*

 RUE power is service. The Pope must serve all people, especially the poor, the weak, the vulnerable. —Pope Francis **JULY 6**

Where is power?

REFLECTION. Since the beginning of recorded history we read of people who have a thirst for power. More often than not their quest for power expresses itself in controlling others.

Pope Francis, reflecting on the example of Jesus, hits the nail on the head that true power expresses itself in service to others. Thank you for your witness to power as expressed through your care and service to others.

PRAYER. *Jesus, my Lord, may I serve joyfully all people, especially those on the margins.*

NLY those able to acknowledge their mistakes and ask pardon receive understanding and forgiveness from others. —Pope Francis

JULY 7

As we forgive others…

REFLECTION. One of the non-negotiables of following Jesus is forgiveness. We need to forgive and to be forgiven. One of the gifts we receive when we ask for forgiveness is humility.

We acknowledge that we are imperfect. In doing so our hearts open up and we realize that all of us on this journey of faith are imperfect and we need each other. Forgive and allow your heart to be open to God's grace.

PRAYER. *O God, may I be generous in my forgiveness and humble in dealing with others.*

 F YOU want to change the world, go home and love your family. —Mother Teresa

JULY 8

It starts at home

REFLECTION. Often we set our sights on how we can travel and serve in order to change the world. There is something alluring about serving others from a foreign culture.

While God may call us to do something radical like this, most of us will spend our time in our home with our own family. This is mission ground for most of us.

PRAYER. *Lord, let me not forget those closest to me when I think about service.*

MISSED you yesterday!

—Ellen Brandt, Teacher

Short and sweet

REFLECTION. What a beautiful sentiment, "I missed you yesterday!" How many of us feel like we don't really matter? Hopefully that's not the case, but the truth is that many people feel this way.

The teacher's four words communicate love! I'm sure God reacts with joy when we reconnect with Him, and I know that others feel valued and loved when we let them know that we missed them.

PRAYER. *Lord, may I use those four simple words often in order to communicate love.*

 EVER bother about people's opinions.

—Mother Teresa

Love, don't judge

REFLECTION. Mother Teresa knew that human beings are easily swayed by what and how other people think. We can quickly judge others based on their political opinions or other points of view and that begins to divide us.

If we are busy judging people than we will not be loving them. Perhaps it's wiser to care for them for who they are and not for what they believe.

PRAYER. *Lord God, thank You for loving me at every age and stage of my life.*

HE command I give you is this: love one another. —Jn 15:17

11

Total gift of self

REFLECTION. In the Greek language there are a few words for love. The one that the Gospel writer chooses is *agape*. This quality of love refers to the total gift of self—nothing held back. This is best exemplified in the person of Jesus.

Jesus gave Himself totally in His three-year ministry and on the Cross. He continues to give Himself in the Eucharist. Continue to model this love in all those you care for.

PRAYER. *Loving God, thank You for holding nothing back in Your love for me.*

 ND you also are my witnesses. —Jn 15:27

JULY

12

Never be afraid to give witness

REFLECTION. More often than not we think of giving witness through our words. Words are important in sharing our faith. How can people believe if they haven't heard of Jesus?

You give witness through your actions each and every day. While you may not always have the words, you certainly can give witness through the love you show to others.

PRAYER. *Jesus, may my actions speak of my deep love for You.*

BUT when the spirit of truth comes, he will guide you into all the truth.
—Jn 16:13

The appealing nature of the truth

REFLECTION. Jesus knew that He would not be able to teach us everything we desired to know while He was with His disciples. Thank God that He did not leave us as orphans!

He has given us the Holy Spirit to guide the Church and to teach us all we need to know for salvation. Pray to the Holy Spirit so that you may know what the truth is. In seeking the truth you will experience freedom.

PRAYER. *Holy Spirit, lead me and all people to know and love the truth.*

ASK and you will receive, so that your joy may be complete.
—Jn 16:24

The prayer of supplication

REFLECTION. Often we don't have what we need because we don't ask for it. We have a loving Father in Heaven who desires the best for us, yet He desires that we come to Him for our needs.

Take some time to reflect upon what your needs may be. Bring these needs before God in prayer for He desires that you have joy—the joy of knowing that God loves you and is with you every step of the way.

PRAYER. *Jesus, may my joy come from You! Help me seek Your will in my life.*

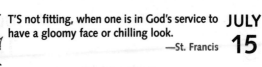

T'S not fitting, when one is in God's service to have a gloomy face or chilling look.
—St. Francis

JULY 15

Lead with joy

REFLECTION. It is said that St. Francis was the most Christ-like person who ever lived. He was open to all and shared the Good News with everyone. He knew that the joy in our heart needs to be expressed in our face and through our hands.

Is the expression on your face reflecting the joy in your heart? Never be afraid to lead with joy when caring for others.

PRAYER. *Jesus, lead me to Your Sacred Heart so I may lead with joy in all I do.*

HE family is where we are formed as people. Every family is a brick in the building of society.
—Pope Francis

JULY 16

Together we can do great things

REFLECTION. When the family breaks down the society breaks down. When we see decay and unrest in society we can almost always point to the breakdown of the family unit.

How were you formed in your family? Were there family meals, time to recreate, time to pray together? What we do as families is extremely important to the well-being of society.

PRAYER. *Lord, let me make time for my family so we may pray, play, and serve together.*

UT take courage! I have overcome the world. —Jn 16:33

God has the last word

REFLECTION. Caregivers are on the front line when tragedy strikes. Whether it's a skinned knee or a major incident, caregivers are there to heal, comfort, and take charge. It can be exhausting.

Yes, there will be suffering. Yes, there will be misunderstanding, but as Catholics we continue to follow our Lord's example of loving service to others.

PRAYER. *Jesus, help me to have courage when I begin to fail and start to lose hope.*

HAVE glorified you on earth by completing the work you entrusted to me. —Jn 17:4

Your work glorifies God

REFLECTION. Jesus followed God's will even when suffering was part of the package. Your work has been entrusted to you by God in the same way. Suffering may be part of the package, but there is joy as well.

Realize that how you do your service is important and valued by God. What do you think is the most important work that God has entrusted to you?

PRAYER. *Lord, may I view the work and service I do as a work entrusted to me by You.*

S YOU sent me into the world, so have I sent them into the world. —Jn 17:18

A mission to accomplish

REFLECTION. Just as Jesus was sent to us with a mission to accomplish, we too, as Catholics, firmly believe that we have a mission. This mission should be modeled after Jesus no matter what profession or state of life we may find ourselves in.

Each day is an opportunity to care for and serve those whom we meet with the same love that we have seen in Christ.

PRAYER. *Jesus, let me see my life as an extension of Your mission and Your work.*

ROM the minute I open the car door in the parking lot I begin to serve.
—John Parker, Teacher

Always ready and prepared

REFLECTION. Often we think that we are "on" from 9 to 5 or whatever the time we begin and leave work. How many opportunities to care and serve and smile occur during the time immediately before and after the time we get paid?

Be open to those unexpected moments before, during, and after work where God may break into our lives. See them as "God moments" and be open to serve.

PRAYER. *Lord, may I seize opportunities to serve even at inconvenient times.*

HE woman said to Peter, "Are you not one of this man's disciples?" He replied, "I am not." —Jn 18:17

JULY 21

Be not afraid to be His disciple

REFLECTION. The Gospels are very honest about the failures of Jesus' disciples. Thomas doubted the resurrection; they all fled from the Cross; and Peter denied that he knew Jesus three times. We are all sinners in need of God's mercy.

As Jesus forgave and sent His Holy Spirit to the disciples we too have that same Spirit. Are you willing to identify with Jesus?

PRAYER. *Jesus, forgive me for those times that I denied You through my words and actions.*

 ND at that very moment, a cock crowed. —Jn 18:27

JULY 22

When we realize we failed

REFLECTION. Like St. Peter, we have all experienced those moments when we realized that we have just blown it. We failed. We missed the mark. We take full responsibility for our failure.

At those times we do what the Saints did, they asked forgiveness and got right back up and tried again. Hopefully a rooster won't crow every time we blow it, but forgiveness is available and we need to move on.

PRAYER. *St. Peter, pray for me that I may be strong in faith and humble when I sin.*

HEN he said to the disciple, "Behold, your mother." —Jn 19:27

23

One of God's greatest gifts to the Church

REFLECTION. Even while dying on the Cross Jesus was thinking of you and desired to comfort you. How did He do this? He did this by giving us the best gift ever—the gift of His mother.

A mother's love extends beyond time and space and can continue to nurture us long after she's gone. Mary's love and care for you continues throughout your life. Turn to her often for she is our Mother and she cares for you.

PRAYER. *Mary, pray for me that I may be strong like you.*

———————————

HEN Peter and the other disciple set out and made their way toward the tomb. —Jn 20:3

JULY
24

What was their reaction?

REFLECTION. On Easter Sunday we read that Mary Magdalene, Peter, and John all went to the tomb. Mary was looking for the body of Jesus. Where is the body of Jesus today? Certainly He is present in the Eucharist, but also He is alive in those whom we serve.

Seek Him and He will make Himself known in the people you care for and serve.

PRAYER. *Risen Lord, may I seek Your face in those I encounter each day.*

LOVE casts out fear, but we have to get over the fear in order to get close enough to love them. —Dorothy Day

What separates us from others?

REFLECTION. Dorothy Day is considered a Saint by those who knew her and saw the love she showed to the poor on the lower East Side of New York. Her quote does give us reason to pause and reflect on why we may be hesitant to reach out to others.

Perhaps we need the eyes of faith to see others, even those who may appear strange to us, as our brothers and sisters in need of love.

PRAYER. *Lord, help me cast off any fear that I may have when it comes to caring for others.*

AFTER saying this, he breathed on them and said, "Receive the Holy Spirit." —Jn 20:22

JULY 26

God's life within us

REFLECTION. While the Holy Spirit is part mystery, we can look at what He has done throughout the Scriptures. Whenever the Holy Spirit shows up He seems to be empowering people for witness.

When we think life has become too much it's then that we need to ask the Holy Spirit to empower us for our work.

PRAYER. *Holy Spirit, Advocate, empower me to accomplish the mission which Jesus has given me.*

PRIDE makes us artificial and humility makes us real. —Thomas Merton

Think less of self

REFLECTION. Humility is not thinking less of self, but of thinking of self less. When pride creeps in we begin to think that we can go it alone and we don't need others or God.

Thomas Merton's insight rings true with those who have ceased being the center of the world and allow room in their lives for God and others. In caring for others, allow time for God and others to care for you as well.

PRAYER. *Jesus, help me to be the person You have called me to be in my service to others.*

LOVE ought to show itself more in deeds than in words. —St. Ignatius of Loyola

Glimpses of the divine

REFLECTION. There are well over 14,000 songs with the word "love" in the title. Love is what we all long for. As beautiful as some of these love songs may be the effect isn't lasting.

Loving actions however, can have a deep and enduring effect which may impact a person or community for years to come. Your actions make a profound difference in the world.

PRAYER. *Jesus, thank You for Your words and actions of love for me and for the world.*

JESUS said to him, "Feed my lambs."
—Jn 21:15

Feed, don't count my lambs

REFLECTION. Jesus is very clear that St. Peter was to "feed His lambs" and not to count them. How many times are we concerned with numbers in our own particular ministry?

What we should be concerned with is "feeding others." This, of course, does not always refer to food, but it can mean "teaching others" or "serving others." Be focused on the person or "lamb" in front of you.

PRAYER. *Jesus, may I be focused on individuals and giving them my best.*

———————————

CONTINUALLY give thanks to my God for you because of his grace that has been granted to you in Christ Jesus. —1 Cor 1:4

People thank God for you!

REFLECTION. St. Paul wrote a couple of letters to the Corinthian church and we see on more than one occasion that they were a wild group—wild but enthusiastic about their newfound faith.

St. Paul will correct some of their outlandish behavior, but he begins with praise, acknowledging the faith granted to them by Jesus. Think of those you give thanks for and consider how many people give thanks for your life.

PRAYER. *Jesus, all I have is a gift from You. May I use these gifts to serve others.*

EXHORT you in the name of our Lord Jesus Christ to be in full agreement with one another and not permit any divisions.

—1 Cor 1:10

Beware of those who bring division

REFLECTION. St. Paul usually divided his letters into two parts in which he teaches about theology and then writes about morality. A common thread that runs throughout all of his letters is his admonition to be of one mind.

Isn't it true that just one person can bring division to the family and workplace and even the country? Be a peacemaker and beware of those who try to divide.

PRAYER. *Lord, use me to help bring peace and harmony where there is discord and division.*

HOPE is what Mary, Mother of God, sheltered in her heart during the darkest time of her life. —Pope Francis

Good Friday afternoon to Sunday morning

REFLECTION. Mary was at the foot of the Cross. She did not abandon her Son in His and her darkest hour. Christian hope is not naive optimism but rather trust in a person: Jesus Christ.

Mary had this hope and so should we. During our darkest hour it can and is difficult to believe. Carry that hope in your heart and be the spark so others can trust in Jesus, too.

PRAYER. *Mary, pray for me that I may shelter your Son Jesus in my own heart.*

WE PROCLAIM Christ crucified.
—1 Cor 1:22

AUG.
2

The message is clear

REFLECTION. Religion can be the cause of much confusion and debate. St. Paul knew as much when he traveled and shared the Gospel. After arguing, debating, and approaching the Greeks from a philosophical perspective without much success he decided to keep his message simple.

In our service let us not forget the main thing which is caring for the people God has given us.

PRAYER. *Lord, may my faith be more about service and less about making my point.*

THE world promises you comfort but you were not made for comfort. You were made for greatness.
—Pope Benedict XVI

AUG.
3

God's view of greatness

REFLECTION. The word greatness conjures up images of trophies, awards, and roaring crowds. We like to honor those who achieve success, but God gives us another perspective.

Greatness, in God's eyes, comes through service, comes through the Cross. Jesus is our example of true greatness, and His life was given over completely to God. What areas might you need to give over to God?

PRAYER. *Lord, let me not be tempted to stray away from Jesus' model of greatness.*

I CAME to you in weakness, in fear, and in great trepidation. —1 Cor 2:3

We move forward despite our fears

REFLECTION. St. Paul was one of the boldest proclaimers of the Gospel the world has ever known. He died a martyr because of his faith in Jesus. In writing to the Church at Corinth he reveals that he was indeed afraid and thought of himself as weak.

We too, who are at times fearful and weak, need to follow St. Paul's lead and move forward in doing the task God has for us.

PRAYER. *St. Paul, I thank God for you. May I follow your example of service to all of God's people.*

 ITHOUT sacrifice there is no love. —St. Maximilian Kolbe

Love puts the other first

REFLECTION. Words can be powerful especially when they are backed up by good example. St. Maximilian did just that for he exchanged his life for another at the Auschwitz concentration camp.

God knows the sacrifices you make each and every day for your family, friends, loved ones, and for those you serve. St. Maximilian was a Saint for how he lived, not for how he died.

PRAYER. *Lord, I praise You for the lives of the Saints and the example they give us.*

115

MY JOB is to inform, not to convince.
— St. Bernadette

AUG.
6

Avoid arguments and divisions

REFLECTION. Speaking the truth in love is truly an act of service. There is a danger in thinking that we are the ones who are in control of what another person thinks and feels. Spending time with others, teaching and informing them is a noble service that we should be engaged in.

Be prayerful and ask the Holy Spirit to make sure you are speaking the truth before you inform others.

PRAYER. *Lord, I rely on Your word and Holy Spirit to help me to inform others of Your love.*

EYE has not seen, ear has not heard, nor has the human heart imagined what God has prepared for those who love him.
— 1 Cor 2:9

AUG.
7

The promise and the hope

REFLECTION. It would seem that the "key" to receiving all that God has in store for us is love. We may not always understand how God works, but love seeks to please the other even when we don't see the big picture. This is the life of faith.

We respond to the love of God by loving Him and loving our neighbor. Thank God for the faith you have been given and for the opportunities to love others.

PRAYER. *Lord, I love You and seek ways to serve Your people.*

116

WHEN the police showed up I knew everything was going to be okay.
—John Cirelli

To protect and serve

REFLECTION. Police, firefighters, and EMTs often show up when humanity is at its weakest. The sight of them can be of great comfort because of their reputation of service and care.

You are most likely a source of joy and comfort to many people. Some will express their appreciation and others may not. Know that God knows and appreciates your care for His people.

PRAYER. *Lord, may I serve without counting the cost or expecting praise from others.*

IN EVERY group or crowd there is always one person who will feel out of place. Reach out to them.
—Shelly Goodness, Teacher

An eye for those on the margins

REFLECTION. Not everyone who stands alone is lonely or isolated. There are some who don't mind standing on the sidelines. Perhaps it's our responsibility, at the very least, to "check in" with them to make sure they are OK.

How many times do we hear of those who are new to a school or workplace and no one reaches out to say hello to them? Be the person who checks on others to make sure they are fine.

PRAYER. *Lord, may I develop an eye for those who may be lonely or isolated so they may know someone cares.*

HE Rosary is my favorite prayer. A marvelous prayer! —St. John Paul II

Praying. . . not saying the Rosary

REFLECTION. The Rosary has been praised by Saints and Popes alike as a means to deepen their prayer life. To the novice it may seem a bit odd to be repeating all of these "Hail Marys."

When one prays the Rosary and meditates on the sacred mysteries they begin to enter the life and experience of Jesus and those who follow Him. Don't just say it, pray it.

PRAYER. *Blessed Mother, may I enter more deeply into the life of Jesus by praying the Rosary.*

N ORDER to purify a soul, Jesus uses whatever instruments he likes. —St. Faustina

All God does He does in love

REFLECTION. Jesus loves us as we are, yet He doesn't want us to remain as we are. He desires that we are constantly moving towards Him and growing in love.

Those who serve and care for others desire the health and welfare of those with various needs who God leads them to. God is at work in you to make you holy.

PRAYER. *Lord, use whatever means necessary to make me like Yourself.*

A N UNSPIRITUAL person refuses to accept what pertains to the Spirit of God. —1 Cor 2:14

A different lens

REFLECTION. Catholics are not necessarily smarter or better than others, but we do view the world through a spiritual lens. God made everything good, so we have a sacramental view that informs us that God can come to us through beauty, truth, and goodness.

Ask the Holy Spirit to continue to enlighten you to the will of God so that you may see others and circumstances through His eyes.

PRAYER. *Holy Spirit, stir within me so I may see others and myself as a means of God's grace.*

B UT we possess the mind of Christ. —1 Cor 2:16

The boldest words in Scripture

REFLECTION. St. Paul was a man on a mission. He had encountered the risen Lord and gave his life to tell others that Jesus was God. In a bold statement he says, "we possess the mind of Christ."

To possess the mind of Christ is to think and discern from the perspective of Jesus. Spend time with Scripture, adoration, and studying the teaching of the Church, and you will develop the mind of Christ.

PRAYER. *Lord, help me see life from Your perspective so I may act like You.*

TAKING some time for yourself to relax and unwind is not a sin.

—Sr. Catherine Caroll

AUG.
14

Care for the caregiver

REFLECTION. Too often we are defined by what we do. We may even feel a constant pressure to work to the point of exhaustion. This, of course, is insanity and leads to burnout.

Jesus took time alone to pray and to retreat from the crowds. As Jesus did, so must caregivers do as well. Treat yourself to time alone, a day at the spa or a walk on the beach, to be refreshed and renewed.

PRAYER. *Jesus, remind me that You, not I, are the Savior of the World and I need time off.*

I PLANTED the seed, and Apollos watered it, but God caused it to grow. —1 Cor 3:6

AUG.
15

We all have a job to do

REFLECTION. We don't have to do God's job, but God has given us a job to do. St. Paul recognized that each person imparts a different gift to the community.

Don't feel that you have to be all things to all people all the time. God has given you particular gifts and talents. Never be jealous of another's gifts because God has given you your own.

PRAYER. *Lord, thank You for my unique set of gifts and talents which I'll use for Your glory.*

FOR we are God's coworkers. —1 Cor 3:9 **AUG. 16**

Called to labor in the world with God

REFLECTION. One of the biggest complaints in the workforce is that of annoying coworkers. Because we are human and sinful we can get on each other's nerves.

St. Paul reminds us that we are coworkers with none other than God Himself who chose us for a great work in this world. Lean on God when times get tough, and remember that He is always on your side.

PRAYER. *Lord, give me patience and help me to be kind to my coworkers.*

PRAY, hope, and don't worry. **AUG. 17**
—St. Padre Pio of Pietrelcina

Easy to say, difficult to live

REFLECTION. The phrase, "Don't worry," is repeated multiple times by Jesus throughout the Gospels. Perhaps Jesus said it so often because He knows our proclivity to worry.

St. Padre Pio adds the words "pray" and "hope" before the phrase "don't worry," so it would be good to take this advice. When you are worrying take time to pray, hope, and trust in God's love.

PRAYER. *Lord, I admit I worry. Remind me of Your love and care in the midst of life's storms.*

IT IS not hard to obey when we love the one whom we obey. —St. Ignatius of Loyola

AUG.
18

To obey is to listen

REFLECTION. The word obedient has a negative connotation in our society. We often think of someone saying "obey, or else." In reality the word conveys a sense of listening to another.

Being obedient to God means first and foremost to listen to Him. St. Ignatius came to know the love of God during his recovery from a battle wound. Take time each day to listen and then act on God's word.

PRAYER. *Jesus, help me to attune my ear and heart to Your word and Holy Spirit.*

YOU cannot be half a saint; you must be a whole saint or no saint at all. —St. Thérèse of Lisieux

AUG.
19

Go all in!

REFLECTION. When playing Texas Hold'em poker there comes a time when you need to go "all in." This means you place all of your chips in the pot and there is no turning back.

St. Thérèse realized at an early age that when it comes to faith in God the only bet is to go all in. No half measures for her or for any Saint. In your life of faith and service go "all in" and trust in Him who cares for you.

PRAYER. *Lord, may I continue moving forward and go "all in" in my dedication to You.*

KNOW well that the greater and more beautiful the work is, the more terrible will be the storms that rage against it. —St. Faustina

AUG.
20

Be prepared for opposition

REFLECTION. The old adage is true that "no good deed goes unpunished." While there is some humor in this we know that there is a power for evil in this world that hates God and all of His works of charity.

Don't be discouraged if your good plans are sabotaged because once our work is given over to God it belongs to Him. Overcome evil with good and entrust all to the Lord.

PRAYER. *Jesus, help me when I become discouraged and overwhelmed by opposition.*

 O YOU not realize that you are God's temple, and that the Spirit of God dwells in you? —1 Cor 3:16

AUG.
21

Treat yourself as God's dwelling place

REFLECTION. Humans have inherent dignity because God became man in the person of Jesus. Christians recognize through their baptism that not only do they have dignity but that God Himself has called us and chosen to dwell in us.

Care for your body, your soul, your mind, and all that you are. Recognize this dignity in others and you will begin treating them as you would treat the Lord.

PRAYER. *God our Father, open my eyes to see Your presence in me and in others.*

MAY never be the smartest person in the room, but I can be the most positive person. **AUG. 22** —Joseph Sprague, Coach

You are in charge of your attitude

REFLECTION. They say that it's your attitude, not your aptitude, which will determine your altitude. How high and far we go in life does depend a lot on our attitude.

If you are the most brilliant person in the room but you are also arrogant, selfish, not a team player,—well, who wants to be around a person like that? How can you be a more positive person?

PRAYER. *Lord, help me to be the person You call me to be so I may be a positive force in the world.*

 ISTEN and attend with the ear of your heart. **AUG. 23** —St. Benedict

Next time, I'll listen with my heart

REFLECTION. The heart is tricky for sometimes it can lead us astray from the right course of action. However, the heart has reason that reason does not always understand.

St. Benedict realized that the life of faith relies on the word of God and His Holy Spirit which continues to speak to our hearts. Attend to these promptings of the Spirit and seek advice before you act on them.

PRAYER. *Lord, may Your voice resonate within my heart and lead me in all of Your ways.*

124

IF IN speaking I use human and angelic **AUG.**
tongues but do not have love, I am nothing
more than a noisy gong. —1 Cor 13:1 **24**

Love is the key

REFLECTION. In St. Paul's day the Greeks valued
the gift and art of speaking philosophically.
Christians had the gift of praying in tongues
through the Holy Spirit. St. Paul reminds them
that any speech done without love accounts for
nothing.

Corinth was the brass-making capital of the
world so the reference to the noisy gong would
have had a real impact. Are your words spoken
in love?

PRAYER. *Lord, I'm sorry for the times I have
spoken without love as the foundation.*

LOVE is patient; love is charitable. **AUG.**
—1 Cor 13:4 **25**

Actions not feelings matter most

REFLECTION. St. Paul is writing to a young
Christian community who were at times more
concerned with who was right than with loving
one another. We can fall into the same trap.

We, as those early Corinthians, must always
set our sight on Jesus as the example of love.
Where might there be opportunities for you to
grow in patience and charity?

PRAYER. *Lord, may I be loving in word and
action so as to reflect Your presence.*

LOVE is never rude, it does not seek its own advantage. —1 Cor 13:5

Sin seeks its own advantage

REFLECTION. The heart, the middle of the words: SIN, PRIDE and LUCIFER is the letter 'I.' Love on the other hand seeks the will and betterment of the other and has little concern for self.

When we put God and others before ourselves we learn what love is and it liberates us from our selfish desires. Who has sought your advantage? Who has loved you in your life?

PRAYER. *Lord, may I look for opportunities to put the needs of others before my own.*

LOVE does not rejoice in wrongdoing but rejoices in the truth. —1 Cor 13:6

Seek truth and it will set you free

REFLECTION. Due to human sin we can rejoice over another's downfall. Loving like Jesus, however, requires us to abandon the old way of being and to seek the truth no matter where it leads.

It can be difficult to speak the truth and at times to face the truth, but ultimately it leads to freedom. We all need someone who can speak the truth in love to us with no fear of repercussions.

PRAYER. *Lord, may I be humble enough to accept the truth and the courage to speak it.*

CHARITY brings to life again those who are spiritually dead.

—St. Thomas Aquinas

AUG. 28

You can raise the dead

REFLECTION. St. Thomas Aquinas is considered the most brilliant theologian to have ever lived. Evidence of his brilliance can be found in his life and his writing.

His observation that an act of charity, love, can bring a spiritually dead person to life is within the grasp of us all. Never discount a person you meet or an act of kindness you extend to them.

PRAYER. *Lord, thank You for including me in Your ministry to bring people back to life.*

LOVE never fails.

—1 Cor 13:8

AUG. 29

God never fails

REFLECTION. What is done out of love never fails and is in fact, eternal. The service and care we give to others has effects that we may never be aware of or see in this lifetime.

In our culture where we use the word "love" as a feeling, we see love come and go. Christian love flows from the heart of God who is love. Let God's love flow through your hands and feet and you will be doing the work of God.

PRAYER. *Jesus, thank You for Your love for me. May I love others with that same, unfailing love.*

127

JOY is very infectious; therefore, be always full of joy.
—Mother Teresa

AUG.
30

Let your joy be a net to catch souls

REFLECTION. Happiness depends on situations whereas joy should be a constant in the life of a believer. Even when life throws obstacles in our way we know that we are not alone.

There is no obstacle that God is not aware of or that can overwhelm us, not even death itself. Let the joy that comes from serving the Lord be evident and lift others above their sorrow.

PRAYER. *Lord, increase my faith and joy especially during difficult times.*

———————

TO CONVERT somebody go and take them by the hand and guide them.
—St. Thomas Aquinas

AUG.
31

One person at a time

REFLECTION. For some Catholics the word "convert" has a negative connotation. We know that we must continually undergo conversion but we are hesitant to "convert" others.

What we are doing is leading others to the person of Jesus. We don't impose our beliefs but rather propose who Jesus is to us. Share your story and be the light that Christ calls us to be.

PRAYER. *Jesus, may I never shy away from speaking about Your love, mercy, and forgiveness.*

B E A good child, and God will help you.   **SEPT.**
                              —St. Joan of Arc

1

The simplicity of the Saints

REFLECTION. St. Joan of Arc is known for her courage on the battlefield. Her simple advice is good to remember for those who serve and care for others who also have "battles" to fight in providing the best for those we care for.

We need to take care of the things we can and then leave the rest to God. In the end, be a good child of God; trust in His divine providence.

PRAYER. *Lord, may I be good and take care of my responsibilities as I entrust all to You.*

 L OOKING in on our town's senior citizens provides basic health checkups and friendship checkups.—Denise Sullivan, R.N.   **SEPT.**

2

You are more than your talents

REFLECTION. The saying goes that you don't have gifts... you are the gift. This implies that while we all have natural talents we are much more than what we can do. We are created in the image and likeness of God so we have inestimable value.

We use our skills for others but who we are is the real gift. Share yourself with those you serve and the relationships will flourish.

PRAYER. *Jesus, may I bring my whole self to those I serve and share myself with them.*

129

E WHO can preserve gentleness amid pains, and peace amid worry and the multitude of affairs, is almost perfect.

SEPT. 3

—St. Francis de Sales

Seeking perfection in our daily life

REFLECTION. Saints are not made by escaping the rigors and difficulties of life but rather by relying on their faith in God in the midst of life's storms. St. Francis de Sales wrote his book, *The Devout Life* specifically for lay people.

Holiness is not only for clergy and religious but for all believers. In what areas do you need to grow in holiness and trust in the Lord?

PRAYER. *Jesus, I'm not a Saint yet I desire to grow in my faith. Help me to be more like You.*

 OWEVER, when I became a man, I put all childish ways aside. —1 Cor 13:11

SEPT. 4

Growing up or growing old

REFLECTION. Near the end of St. Paul's great description of love he reflects on his own actions and attitudes and says that he put "childish ways aside." We are certainly called to be childlike in our faith and trust in the Lord but not "childish."

As we mature in faith we will realize that serving others and continuing to grow in our faith helps put childish ways aside.

PRAYER. *Lord, help me to grow in my faith and trust in You as I mature in my faith.*

THUS there are three things that endure: faith, hope, and love, and the greatest of these is love. —1 Cor 13:13

What will last after we've gone?

REFLECTION. When people reach a certain age they begin to think about their legacy. What will they leave behind? Catholics look to Jesus for this answer and reflect on His legacy of love as expressed in service, forgiveness, and sacrifice. These expressions of love are available to all.

How are you building on your legacy each day through your faith, hope, and love?

PRAYER. *My God, keep my eyes focused on love and not on the temporal things of this world.*

DO NOT let anyone lead you astray. "Bad company corrupts good morals." —1 Cor 15:33

Be with others who are faithful

REFLECTION. Catholics are to witness to the love of God to those who don't know Him. This means that we should show others the way of Jesus no matter how off the straight and narrow they may be.

Be careful however, not to be led astray by those who are not following the way of Christ. Be grounded and surrounded by friends who have the mind of Christ.

PRAYER. *Holy Spirit, protect me from those who do not have my best interests at heart.*

131

NDEED, the stars differ among themselves in splendor. —1 Cor 15:41

SEPT. 7

We all can reflect the splendor of God

REFLECTION. St. Paul uses everything he can to encourage the Corinthians to value each and every person. He writes about the sun, the moon, human and animal bodies, and even the stars.

In a sense, you are a star! You have Christ's presence within you and you shine the brightest when you serve and put Christ's love for others into action. Shine brightly today and every day!

PRAYER. *Holy Spirit, shine the love and light of Christ through my actions today.*

N THE Lord your labor is not in vain. — 1 Cor 15:58

SEPT. 8

Nothing escapes His loving glance

REFLECTION. When we have made the decision to give our lives to Christ we can begin to live our lives "in the Lord." This means that our lives are an extension of God's grace.

We don't compartmentalize our lives and think only of Sunday as the Lord's day, but all we do and who we are belong to Jesus. You are needed and necessary to do the work of God.

PRAYER. *Lord, remind me that my work, no matter how small, should be done with love.*

132

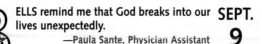

ELLS remind me that God breaks into our lives unexpectedly.

—Paula Sante, Physician Assistant

SEPT. 9

Where has God broken into your life?

REFLECTION. There was a time when villages relied on bells to call people to church and to set forth the hours of the day. There are still a few pious people who pause and pray the Angelus when they hear the bells at noon.

Bells can remind us that God entered into time to redeem humankind. May they remind you that God continues to break into our lives in unexpected ways.

PRAYER. *Jesus, may I be open to You breaking into my life to remind me that You are still active.*

CCORDING to Scripture, it is the heart that prays.

—St. Joseph's Guide to the Catechism

SEPT. 10

Heart to heart in prayer

REFLECTION. In times of stress, words can escape us. The Catholic Church has passed on many beautiful formal prayers which can be an aid to us when our own words fail. It is not necessarily words that move the heart of God but rather our heart.

Take time each day to pray and read Scripture, and other devotions, but take time in silence so your heart can speak to His.

PRAYER. *Mary, Mother of God, attune my heart to the Sacred Heart of your Son.*

133

KEEP alert; stand firm in the faith; be courageous; be strong. —1 Cor 16:13

Words of encouragement

REFLECTION. St. Paul knew he would not always be physically present to the community at Corinth so he offers them some advice. Due to human nature, there is a tendency to give a half-hearted effort to our faith.

Remember, our time on earth is limited and we each have a gift to impart to others. Give with a generous heart and stand firm.

PRAYER. *Lord, may I care for others the way You care for me.*

EVERYTHING that you do should be done in love. —1 Cor 16:14

From the greatest to the smallest

REFLECTION. One of the beautiful aspects of the Catholic faith is that every action, from the greatest to the least, can be an occasion to express our faith when we do it with love.

Thank you for doing what you do with love. While you may not be thanked every day, God knows the ways you care for and serve His people. You are a light in a world of darkness.

PRAYER. *Lord, be with those whose work goes mostly unnoticed and who don't realize their worth.*

E CAN all think of a teacher, coach, or neighbor who we owe a debt of thanks. —Frank Borgoto

SEPT. 13

Who do you think of?

REFLECTION. We are most fortunate if we are able to let those people who have been influential in our lives know how much they have meant to us. A card, phone call, or an invitation to lunch to let them know their impact on our lives can mean the world to them.

If those people are no longer with us then we can pay it forward by treating others well and create our own legacy.

PRAYER. *Jesus, may I never be stingy in my appreciation towards others who have helped me.*

GIVE thanks to my God every time I think of you. —Phil 1:3

SEPT. 14

A grateful heart for others

REFLECTION. Who do you think of when the question is posed: "Who has cared for you?" St. Paul must have asked himself that question many times throughout his tumultuous life. He was shipwrecked, beaten, and even left for dead.

He gave thanks to God and so should we. Just think of how many people may be thanking God for your care and presence in their lives.

PRAYER. *Lord, may I be consistent in thanking You for the blessings I receive every day.*

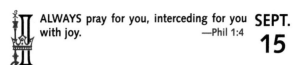

ALWAYS pray for you, interceding for you with joy. —Phil 1:4

Does prayer really matter?

REFLECTION. For those who do not believe in God, the movement of the heart to God through prayer seems like a waste of time. After all, bad things still happen to good people.

The gift of faith and the words and example of Jesus make one thing crystal clear: prayer matters. While it may not change the circumstances, it does change and strengthen us especially when life is difficult. Pray always.

PRAYER. *Holy Spirit, stir within me often so I may pray always and rely on God for all.*

AM confident of this: the one who began a good work in you will bring it to completion on the day of Christ Jesus. —Phil 1:6

Finish your race strong

REFLECTION. The faith that we were baptized in and have grown into during our adulthood is still calling us to move forward. God has created you for a reason and purpose.

Be faithful in living your life according to Christ's call. Love, serve, and care for others as you complete your race of faith.

PRAYER. *Lord, I do not see the end; I'm not always sure why I am here. Guide my steps each day.*

ND for this I pray: that your love may increase ever more. —Phil 1:9

A full and overflowing heart

REFLECTION. While our hearts are relatively small they can certainly overflow. Like a small cup beneath a towering waterfall, our hearts stand beneath the grace and love of God the Father overflowing into the world.

Our responsibility is to stay close to God so that His love may flow through us and then out to the world through service to others.

PRAYER. *Christ Jesus, I love You. May the love I receive from You overflow into my actions.*

T IS simply impossible to lead, without the aid of prayer, a virtuous life.
—St. John Chrysostom

Does virtue still matter?

REFLECTION. Human virtues are firm attitudes, stable dispositions, habitual perfections of intellect and will that govern our actions, order our passions, and guide our conduct according to reason and faith according to the *Catechism of the Catholic Church.*

Prayer is the key habit of a virtuous person for it connects us with the Holy Spirit who empowers us to live a life of loving service.

PRAYER. *Come Holy Spirit, assist me in living a virtuous life of service to others.*

PRUDENCE is the virtue that disposes practical reason to discern our true good in every circumstance.

SEPT. 19

—*Catechism of the Catholic Church*, 1806

Help in discerning what is good

REFLECTION. Faith and reason go hand in hand. The problem arises when we try to discern the good in situations where the good to be achieved is not clear.

While perfection only exists in heaven, we can certainly use both reason and faith to make our decisions. What we may see as caring may not always be best for the other person involved. Think, pray, and then act entrusting all to God.

PRAYER. *Jesus, guide me in making prudent decisions especially when others are involved.*

———————————

OUR Lord needs from us neither great deeds nor profound thoughts; neither intelligence nor talents. He cherishes simplicity.

SEPT. 20

—St. Thérèse of Lisieux

We all need to take a deep breath and relax

REFLECTION. Perhaps it's part of our DNA to desire to do our best and constantly strive to exceed what has been done before. In our life of faith we can earnestly desire to please God which is a good thing.

What St. Thérèse assures us of is that God desires simplicity. Let us not make life or faith too complicated. Slow down. Serve with love.

PRAYER. *Jesus, slow me down in order to focus on the things that really matter in life.*

THE Most Blessed Sacrament is Christ made visible. The poor sick person is Christ again made visible.

SEPT. **21**

—St. Gerard Majella

Where do you see Christ?

REFLECTION. Catholics have great reverence for the real presence of Jesus in the Eucharist. When the priest elevates the Host, the people kneel in humble adoration. Do we give similar reverence to those we meet who are in need?

Perhaps this slight change of perspective from St. Gerard Majella can help guide not only who we serve, but the love and care with which we serve.

PRAYER. *St. Gerard, may I be humble and sensitive to Christ's presence in others as you were.*

WHO except God can give you peace? Has the world ever been able to satisfy the heart?

SEPT. **22**

—St. Gerard Majella

A peace that the world cannot give

REFLECTION. One of the marks of the presence of God is peace. Even in the midst of a difficult situation those who have a relationship with God know that they don't walk alone.

Due to your relationship with God you bring His light wherever you go. Be the light and bring the peace of God to others.

PRAYER. *Jesus, help me to share Your peace and Your love by staying close to You.*

HE WHO died in place of us is the one object of my quest. He who rose for our sakes is my one desire.

SEPT. 23

—St. Ignatius of Antioch

My one desire

REFLECTION. St. Ignatius was one of the early Christians who was born in the decades after the death and resurrection of Jesus. His desire and quest is clear. We need not run to a monastery in the desert to live the same way.

Like St. Ignatius, we live out our vocation in the midst of the world surrounded by our family and friends, serving and caring for those whom God brings our way.

PRAYER. *Lord God, show me ways to seek You in the midst of my family and work life.*

I AM not capable of doing big things, but I want to do everything, even the smallest things, for the greater glory of God.

SEPT. 24

—St. Dominic Savio

Give everything over to the love of God

REFLECTION. A common thread in the lives of the Saints is that so many of them saw great value in doing little things with love. It wasn't the number of people they converted that made them Saints but the love they shared.

Ask God for His perspective as you go about your day. Offer even the smallest of things as an offering to God.

PRAYER. *St. Dominic, pray for me that I may be faithful in performing small acts with great love.*

FOR to me, to live is Christ and to die is gain. —Phil 1:21

A divergent perspective

REFLECTION. Imagine someone saying that to die is to gain. We might think they are in need of some psychological help. However, when we reflect on what we believe, we realize that St. Paul is right. Our physical death is a great loss but we gain heaven, our true home.

Use your time on earth to be good, to do good, and to be a power for good as a true son or daughter of the Father.

PRAYER. *Jesus, may I use my time on earth doing good and following Your way of love.*

ONLY live in a manner worthy of the gospel of Christ. —Phil 1:27

Set your sights on what is above

REFLECTION. Most soldiers, police officers, nurses and firefighters take great pride in their uniform and what it took to qualify for their work. They realize that they represent something greater than themselves especially while in uniform.

Our Christian uniform is our baptismal garment, and it was purchased by Jesus' death on the Cross. Wear it well.

PRAYER. *Mary, Mother of Jesus, pray that I may model my life and actions after your Son.*

THE proof of love is in the works. Where love exists, it works great things. But when it ceases to act, it ceases to exist.

—St. Gregory the Great

Words can be cheap

REFLECTION. In English the word "love" is used to convey a strong affection for anything from pizza to one's family. Other languages have words which are more specific to what love actually is.

Whether or not one uses the correct word, all people can recognize the actions of love which are proven through their works. Who has loved you by their works of service and care?

PRAYER. *Jesus, may my love for others be expressed through loving service.*

WE MUST pray without ceasing, that prayer which is rather a habit of lifting up the heart to God as in a constant communication with Him.

—St. Elizabeth Ann Seton

Weave prayer into all you do

REFLECTION. It can be so easy to compartmentalize our faith. Sundays are for church and prayer is for meals and bedtime. The Saints teach us to integrate our faith with our work.

The way you serve others, the tenderness with which you speak, and the love you put into all you do is an expression of faith which can be prayer. Make your life a prayer.

PRAYER. *Jesus, help me to see all I do as an expression of my love for You.*

HOSE whose hearts are pure are temples of the Holy Spirit. —St. Lucy

The pure in heart will see God

REFLECTION. When friends or guests come over to visit we usually make a mad scramble to make sure our house is clean. We can drive others crazy with our desire to put things in order.

The Holy Spirit desires to make His home in our heart. How can we ensure a proper place for Him to reside? We can ask God to purify our hearts so He has a place to dwell.

PRAYER. *Come Holy Spirit, cleanse me of sin so my heart is pure.*

ANCTIFY yourself and you will sanctify society. —St. Francis of Assisi

Start where you can

REFLECTION. It's a great temptation to throw up our hands and blame "society" for all of its ills. We can rant and rave and tell others what needs to be fixed, and fail to see the sin in our own life.

Certainly we should be proactive when we see injustice, but as people of faith we should take St. Francis' advice and start with ourselves. What do you need to sanctify in your life?

PRAYER. *Lord, reveal to me where I need to grow in faith so I may better serve You.*

THE Lord comes to find another heaven which is infinitely dearer to him—the heaven of our souls, created in His Image, the living temples of the Adorable Trinity. —St Thérèse of Lisieux

Christ dwells in us

REFLECTION. What a beautiful truth: we are created in the image and likeness of God. Through the Eucharist Christ comes to dwell within us, and as Catholics we kneel at His presence.

What a beautiful perspective to have of those we care for. To see others as they truly are, created in the image of God. How different would our interactions be if we always lived this truth.

PRAYER. *Lord, open the eyes of my heart to see Your presence in those I serve and care for.*

DO NOTHING out of selfish ambition or vanity, but humbly regard others as better than yourselves. —Phil 2:3

Look out for others and help raise them up

REFLECTION. St. Paul writes about doing things out of selfish ambition because there were people he knew who acted this way. If you have ever had anyone use you to advance their own cause you know how damaging this behavior can be.

Right and proper behavior gets noticed and has its own reward. Seek to serve others and leave the rest to God who will take up your cause.

PRAYER. *Lord, come to my aid and teach me to have pure motives so as to lift others up.*

ET your attitude be identical to that of Christ Jesus. —Phil 2:5

OCT. 3

Know Christ in order to be like Him

REFLECTION. When was the last time you studied your faith or went a little deeper in your study of Jesus. Adults continue to grow in the knowledge of their profession, but often their religious education stops around eighth grade.

As a caregiver, in order to have the attitude of Christ, we need to spend time with Him and to grow in our knowledge of our faith. The benefits will extend to everyone you know.

PRAYER. *Merciful God, give me a desire to grow in knowledge and love of You.*

ET us run to Mary, and, as her little children, cast ourselves into her arms with a perfect confidence. —St. Francis de Sales

OCT. 4

Am I not your mother?

REFLECTION. Some of our Protestant brothers and sisters don't understand our relationship with Mary. As Jesus honored His mother and father, we too, honor the mother of God.

We may be able to explain theologically the role of Mary in salvation history, but it's just as important to spend time asking for her intercession. All the Saints have this common thread; they knew the love Mary has for us.

PRAYER. *Mary, be a mother to me as I ask for your intercession for the needs in my life.*

145

ACTIONS speak louder than words; let your words teach and your actions speak. —St. Anthony of Padua

What do your actions reveal?

REFLECTION. When Jesus talks about the final judgment He says that those who will receive the Kingdom of God feed the hungry, clothe the naked, and live out the corporal works of mercy.

Take some time to reflect on your actions. Filling up sippy cups, changing diapers, and providing for sick family members all constitute these works of mercy.

PRAYER. *Jesus, may my actions serve as an example of my faith in You.*

IF WE wish to make any progress in the service of God we must begin every day of our life with new eagerness.
—St. Charles Borromeo

A new day, a new beginning

REFLECTION. How often does the groove we get into fall into a rut? Old patterns and ways of living can be ingrained in our behavior making change difficult. The advice of St. Charles Borromeo gives us hope that we can change and even make progress in the spiritual life.

Ask the Holy Spirit to enlighten you each morning and approach each day as an opportunity to be used by God in the service of others.

PRAYER. *Lord, I eagerly await Your will for me and seek to serve You in the world.*

ATHER, he emptied himself, taking the form of a slave. —Phil 2:7

If Jesus can do it so can we

REFLECTION. This passage is often called the "kenosis" which means "emptying." Jesus humbled Himself and became one of us, true God and true man.

If Jesus humbled Himself so must we. Thank you for the ways you have humbled yourself and taken on the role of a "slave" in your care for God's people.

PRAYER. *Lord, may I always look to You for inspiration and guidance on how to live.*

OLD your eyes on God and leave the doing to him. That is all the doing you have to worry about.
—St. Jeanne de Chantal

But Lord, You don't understand…

REFLECTION. How different are the Saints from us! They seem to have reached a point in their lives where they trust in the providence of God with reckless abandon. Most of us worry too much and hold our concerns with a tight grip.

Ask for the Holy Spirit to help you release your grip and present your concerns to God. Trust in Him and stay close to our Father who loves us.

PRAYER. *Jesus, release me from the worries that I hold on to so that I may have peace.*

147

Y ELEMENTARY school teacher, **OCT.**
"Mr. D," had a profound impact on **9**
my future career. —Josh D'Angelo

We may not know whose lives we touch

REFLECTION. Teachers at all levels impart knowledge to their students. Some teachers give information, others provide inspiration, and yet still others are the cause of transformation.

What separates the good from the great? More often than not it's not how smart others are but how much personal attention they give. Think of those lives you have left for the better.

PRAYER. *Lord, on Your short time on earth You made an eternal impact. Help me do the same.*

OR it is God who is at work in you, **OCT.**
enabling you both to desire and to act for **10**
his chosen purpose. —Phil 2:13

God will not impose Himself on our free will

REFLECTION. The Philippian community that St. Paul was writing to was obedient to the word of God and followed St. Paul's teaching—unlike the Galatians who slipped back into old ways.

We, like those Philippians, have the desire to grow in faith and act for His purpose. Realize that the desire to care and serve others comes from God and He is not done with you yet.

PRAYER. *Lord, may I remember that it is Your Holy Spirit at work in me as I care for others.*

THE most powerful weapon to conquer the devil is humility.

OCT.
11

—St. Vincent de Paul

Be humble as a servant of Christ

REFLECTION. It's interesting how the devil can use the good things we do as an opportunity to ruin us. It can be easy to accept the praise of others for a job well done and we should accept that praise as a servant of Christ.

God has given me life and the opportunity to serve, so thanks be to God. When we exclude God from the picture, pride finds an opening.

PRAYER. *Lord, may the only praise I seek come from You for doing Your will with my life.*

DO EVERYTHING without grumbling or arguing.

OCT.
12

—Phil 2:14

Is this really possible?

REFLECTION. Who among us has never argued or grumbled? It almost seems part of our nature to start or join in a good argument, and when we have to do a task we don't like grumbling is not far behind.

St. Paul's advice is worth considering for Jesus is our example and arguments and grumbling rarely advance the Kingdom of God. Be the one who unites others and works joyfully.

PRAYER. *Lord, make me humble like You, so I may serve with a joy-filled heart.*

149

N THE same way, you too must rejoice and
share your joy with me. —Phil 2:18

Let others know of the good things of God

REFLECTION. Most people share good news with
ease and spontaneity. Too often those who have
a relationship with God through Jesus keep our
"God moments" to ourselves.

We see what God is doing in our lives, but
somehow we've been conditioned to keep it to
ourselves. Take a step of faith and share the good
things of God with others with joy.

PRAYER. *Heavenly Father, let the joy of my heart
be shared through the words of my mouth.*

 ART of caring means that the other
allows you to care for them.
—Louis Beauregard

Allow yourself to be cared for

REFLECTION. Caregivers often find themselves
in situations where they face resistance in providing care for others. Do the best you can when
and where you can in those situations.

Remember too, that we all are in need of care,
even you. Be open to receive humbly the care
offered to you. They may be God's angels sent to
you.

PRAYER. *Lord, You allowed others to serve You
during Your life, may I do the same.*

REMEMBER to care for yourself. You can't pour from an empty cup.

OCT.
15

—Therese Murphy, R.N.

Who's filling your cup?

REFLECTION. Sometimes you need just one good "well" to draw from that will sustain you in a life of service. Maybe that "well" is your spouse or your relationship with God. Others have various wells that they draw from in order to be grounded and supported as they care for others.

What or who nourishes your faith and supports you along the way?

PRAYER. *Lord, thank You for those who give me strength along life's journey.*

I HAVE no one else like him in his genuine concern for your welfare.

OCT.
16

—Phil 2:20

The gift of reliable people

REFLECTION. They say that everyone should have a St. Paul in their lives and everyone should have a Timothy—someone to mentor and someone to be mentored by.

Who has guided you along the way and been there for good counsel? Who is someone you can always rely on and perhaps mentor? Seek out good role models and don't be afraid to take someone under your wings.

PRAYER. *St. Timothy, pray that I may be as faithful and reliable as you.*

151

IKE a son helping his father, he has worked with me in the service of the gospel. —Phil 2:22

Brothers and sisters in the Lord

REFLECTION. There is something about being on a mission that brings people together in a unique way. An individual's background, race, or age seems to matter little when people are all headed in the same direction.

In your work and vocation as a caregiver you have a higher calling as a Catholic for we serve not for a paycheck alone but for the service of the Gospel.

PRAYER. *Jesus, thank You for the people in my life who serve because of their faith.*

 ECEIVE him joyfully in the Lord, and value people like him very highly. —Phil 2:29

Value people, not things

REFLECTION. The most important things in life are not things but people and the friendship and relationships they provide. When St. Paul's community was suffering, he sent people to them.

Think of the many people you have been sent to and have ministered to. Never forget how highly God regards you and your service to His people. You are a gift to many.

PRAYER. *Heavenly Father, may I receive all people as being sent by You.*

O ONE heals himself by wounding another. —St. Ambrose

19

Put an end to violence

REFLECTION. Caregivers are often on the front line where others have been hurt by violence. Domestic abuse, rioting, shootings all require someone to step in to heal and to care.

In these situations your loving presence can speak volumes. Speak of Jesus. Speak of His mercy and forgiveness to those who are tempted to retaliate with violence. Model for them the love of Christ.

PRAYER. *Lord God, may I to speak of forgiveness and in humility ask for forgiveness.*

 OTHING is far from God. —St. Monica

OCT.

20

His reach is enough

REFLECTION. St. Monica is remembered for her faithfulness in praying for the conversion of her son St. Augustine. Statues depicting the face of St. Monica will often have deep circles below her eyes signifying the years she spent praying for him and the tears she shed.

Be faithful in your service, but also be faithful in prayer. Entrust all to God who can reach all people and situations.

PRAYER. *Lord, may my prayer be always before Your throne of grace.*

FINALLY, my brethren, rejoice in the Lord.
—Phil 3:1

There is cause for rejoicing!

REFLECTION. St. Paul was not blind to the struggles and persecution of the early Christian church. Yet in the midst of the struggles he reminds the Philippians to rejoice. In fact, St. Paul most likely wrote his letter from prison.

When the Lord is truly the Lord of our lives we can have hope even when everything seems bleak. You are the cause of many people's rejoicing for how you serve.

PRAYER. *Jesus, remind me often that all will be well when I trust in You.*

BEWARE of evildoers!
—Phil 3:2

Evil is a reality

REFLECTION. Evil exists. It was true in Jesus' day and it's true today. While you are being the "light of the world" through your service, take St. Paul's warning and beware of those who do evil. They may come to you with a smile but by their fruits you will know them.

Do they gossip, slander, divide, and treat people as objects or steppingstones? Avoid them and focus on your mission.

PRAYER. *Holy Spirit, enlighten me and protect me from those who do harm.*

BUT I press on to take hold of that for which Christ once took hold of me. —Phil 3:12

OCT.
23

Run the good race

REFLECTION. How often have we witnessed someone or even ourselves suffer "burnout" on the job? The lack of joy in their lives overflows to everything they are involved in.

Recognize the signs of "burnout" in your life and take steps to care for yourself along the way. Cling to Jesus who is the source of our strength and He will refresh you.

PRAYER. *Mary, Mother of God, may I press on knowing that caring and serving is God's will.*

CHARITY is that with which no man is lost, and without which no man is saved. —St. Robert Bellarmine

OCT.
24

Above all...love

REFLECTION. Charity is that virtue which we call love. The quality of love that is best expressed in the person of Jesus Christ, who laid down His life for others. Easy to say; difficult to do.

Christians have been following Jesus' way of love for close to two thousand years, leaving an example through the lives of the Saints. Do all you do in charity and you will become Christlike.

PRAYER. *Lord, may I love like You and never count the cost.*

BRETHREN, join in imitating me.

—Phil 3:17

OCT.
25

Would you want others to imitate you?

REFLECTION. More than once in the New Testament does St. Paul use himself as an example of Christian conduct. While most of us have some very good qualities to imitate, it does give us pause to reflect on all areas of our lives.

When we are tired, angry, and upset, do we want others to imitate us? Pray, reflect, and have the courage to act.

PRAYER. *Lord God, may I allow Your presence to shine through my behavior.*

BUT our citizenship is in heaven.

—Phil 3:20

OCT.
26

Our true home

REFLECTION. A great deal is made of patriotism and having pride in one's country and rightly so. Many accomplishments and sacrifices have been made by the founders of most great nations.

While we may tend to fix our eyes on our own country, Catholics have their main citizenship in Heaven. This eternal perspective may help give meaning to our purpose on earth.

PRAYER. *Jesus, You are my Lord and God. Help me to be worthy of being a citizen in Your kingdom.*

E WHO trusts himself is lost. He who trusts in God can do all things.

—St. Alphonsus Liguori

I was lost but now I am found

REFLECTION. Jesus asks us to trust in His love and mercy for our salvation and for all of our needs. We say as much each time we pray the "Our Father."

How do we show we trust Him? We live our lives each day praying for His guidance, asking for our daily needs, and trusting that whatever befalls us is part of His divine plan, empowered by the Holy Spirit to love and serve others.

PRAYER. *Come Holy Spirit, reveal to me areas of my life I have not yet surrendered to God.*

ET your kindness be known to everyone.

—Phil 4:5

Not knowledge but kindness

REFLECTION. Too often we judge people by the degree or title they have. These, of course, are not bad in themselves, but we can place too much emphasis on their importance.

Who is the kindest person you know? Who has been kind in good times and in bad? Seek out opportunities to be kind, and you will be the light of Christ.

PRAYER. *Christ, Light of the world, shine in me and through me in every act of kindness I show.*

UR wish, our object, our chief preoc-
cupation must be to form Jesus in ourselves. —St. John Eudes

OCT. 29

Whose image are you conformed to?

REFLECTION. As a child I used to imitate the bat-
ting stances of my favorite baseball players, and
I would paint my hockey mask the same style as
my favorite goaltender to be like them.

Christ desires to be one with you and to make
your heart His home. Before we "work" on ourselves, we need to ask Christ to enter into our
lives to care and serve others as He did.

PRAYER. *Merciful Lord, may my heart be conformed to Your Sacred Heart.*

 O NOT worry about anything, but
present your needs to God in prayer
and petition. —Phil 4:6

OCT. 30

Open your heart and give God your burden

REFLECTION. St. Paul knew firsthand that the life
of a Christian was full of danger and potential
anxiety. His advice was good two thousand years
ago, and it's still good today.

Give your worry to God. Pray, pray, and pray
some more, letting our Father know what's worrying you. Let others know as well that they don't
need to carry their burden alone; God cares.

PRAYER. *Lord, let me speak of the gift of prayer
to others and offer to pray for and with them.*

THEN the peace of God . . . will guard your hearts and your minds in Christ Jesus. —Phil 4:7

Cause and effect

REFLECTION. What is the effect of casting your cares on God through prayer? St. Paul tells us the result will be peace. This peace comes because we know our Father's love. We have seen it displayed on the Cross of Jesus, so we take hope and rest assured in God's sovereign love.

Pray for those you care for and be assured that God the Father is caring for you.

PRAYER. *Lord, let me know of Your love especially when I am at the edge of despair.*

OURS is the Spirit of the Eucharist, the total gift of self. —St. Katharine Drexel

Behold, the Lamb of God

REFLECTION. There is no greater gift than the gift of self. In the Eucharist we not only adore Christ but we receive Him.

The reception of Holy Communion is not just a once-a-week event but an ongoing way of life for those who are in communion with Jesus. We receive Him and then we can give Him to the world through our loving service to others.

PRAYER. *Jesus, may my reception of You in the Eucharist lead to greater love for others.*

YOU were, of course, concerned for me, but you had no opportunity to show it.
—Phil 4:10

Make your concern known

REFLECTION. Caring people are always looking to show concern for others. With or without words there are ample ways to put our care into action so others may know we are thinking of them.

Letters, cards, text messages, and phone calls are ways we can keep in touch with those we care about. Just letting them know we care is often enough.

PRAYER. *Lord, I thank You for coming in the flesh to reveal how much You care for us.*

I CAN do all things through Christ who strengthens me.
—Phil 4:13

His strength in you is enough

REFLECTION. We should admire St. Paul for the way he handled the hardships and abuse he endured during his preaching ministry. He experienced God's grace working through him daily.

All of us face hardships as well. Perhaps not being shipwrecked or beaten with rods, but we have all endured some physical, financial, and emotional suffering. His grace is still enough.

PRAYER. *Jesus, strengthen my faith through whatever hardship I endure.*

THEY are a fragrant offering, an acceptable sacrifice pleasing to God.

—Phil 4:18

Good works do matter

REFLECTION. When the Romans conquered an enemy they made their captives march back to Rome and before them was a cauldron of sweet-smelling incense. For the Romans it signified victory.

Your good deeds in caring for others and spreading the love of Christ have the same effect before the throne of God. Every good work is pleasing and acceptable in His sight.

PRAYER. *Holy Spirit, comfort me and others whom I care for and serve.*

PRAYER purifies us; reading instructs us.

—St. Isidore of Seville

Feed your heart and mind

REFLECTION. The Saints have a way of simplifying things and putting the mysteries of God in words that all can reflect on. What are you filling your mind with?

The temptation is to spend our time watching TV or scrolling through our newsfeed on our electronic devices and get distracted from what really matters. Feed your mind and heart with the things of God.

PRAYER. *St. Isidore, pray that I may focus on what really matters in life.*

YOU must never ask Jesus to wait.
—St. Ursula

NOV.
6

I am ready Lord

REFLECTION. There are a few people in the Gospels who had encounters with Jesus but would not follow Him. Their plans superseded His plans.

We must avoid putting our needs ahead of God's will, and be attentive to what God may ask. If we are praying, seeking God's will, and serving others we are most likely on the right path.

PRAYER. *Lord, may my response to serving You always be "yes!"*

THIS is important: to get to know people, listen, and expand the circle of ideas.
—Pope Francis

NOV.
7

Collaborate and listen

REFLECTION. One might assume that the Pope has all the answers to all the problems of the world and seeks only his own counsel. Pope Francis knows the value of collaboration and working together for the good.

In your efforts to serve, think about all the others involved in the process. Listen, share, and together you can do something more beautiful for the Lord.

PRAYER. *Jesus, may I work together with others to bring justice and love into the world.*

E HAVE heard of your faith in Christ Jesus and of the love that you have for all the saints.

NOV. 8

—Col 1:4

God knows and cares about your work

REFLECTION. Often our reputations precede us. How glorious it is that God knows of your love and faith in His son!

Try to imagine all the people that you have impacted for the good throughout your life. We may focus on those times we failed, but we should rejoice in the fact that God knows about our work in caring and being present to others.

PRAYER. *My Lord and my God, may the care I give always reflect back on You.*

 AY you be fortified with the strength that comes from his glorious power.

NOV. 9

—Col 1:11

Power from on high

REFLECTION. Eating healthy can fortify the mind and body and getting enough exercise strengthens us as well. As people of faith, we often work and operate in conditions which aren't always "Christian."

We need the power that comes from our relationship with God and His Holy Spirit. When giving of yourself, turn to the Holy Spirit often and ask for His power.

PRAYER. *Holy Spirit, empower me to continue to do the work of God faithfully.*

ERVING others enables me to go beyond my own needs so that I can see and respond to the needs of others.

—Michael Vyskocil

Act loud with your actions

REFLECTION. Caring people seem to act spontaneously as the need arises and not out of obligation. Like Jesus, we need to respond to needs as they arise even when it is inconvenient.

This selfless attitude becomes natural over time and it makes it easy for others to discern who the caring people are. Pray that your service becomes a natural part of who you are.

PRAYER. *Lord, each day open my ears, eyes, and heart to the basic needs of those around me.*

 N THE shoes of the other, we learn to have a great capacity for understanding.

—Pope Francis

With age comes wisdom

REFLECTION. What does it mean to walk in the shoes of others? It means at the very least, to consider the other person's circumstances and perspective.

We may be able to do that from the comfort of our couch, but until we journey a few steps out in the real world with them we won't really understand. Take the risk to accompany others on their journey.

PRAYER. *Lord Jesus, give me an empathetic heart to journey with others and not to judge them.*

I AM a sinner and I am fallible.

—Pope Francis

NOV.
12

We all need God's mercy

REFLECTION. Psychologists tell us that there is a side to ourselves that is hidden from us. While we may remain a mystery to ourselves, one thing that we can recognize is that we too, like Pope Francis, are sinners.

Although loved by God, we are still fallible at times. Rejoice that God loves you and works through you anyway.

PRAYER. *Merciful God, may my joy in caring be rooted in a deep sense of Your love.*

LET us bring God's tender caress to others, to those who are in need. —Pope Francis

NOV.
13

Last caress

REFLECTION. The last caress of Jesus' life was wrought with violence: His death on the Cross. Yet, through this action God sealed His tender and redemptive love for us.

Can we refuse to do any less? Who is in need in your family, home, neighborhood or workplace? You need not seek the poor in faraway places for more often than not they are on our doorstep.

PRAYER. *Abba, Father, may I always give of myself with a full and generous heart.*

I F YOU have God at the center of all your actions you will achieve your goals.
—Blessed Pier G. Frassati

**NOV.
14**

Not just on Sundays

REFLECTION. Some people relegate their faith to a Sunday service. While this is important, our faith should overflow into all aspects of our life. Our family, sport, social, and work should all be infused by our faith.

When we do so our faith becomes much more than a Sunday obligation but a lifestyle of loving service for all.

PRAYER. *Lord, forgive me those times when I have pushed You to the sidelines.*

HEN God is with us we don't have to be afraid of anything.
—Blessed Pier G. Frassati

**NOV.
15**

God is always with us

REFLECTION. When fear strikes a child the first thing they do is cry out for their mom and dad. We too, even as adults, experience moments of fear and of life's fragile uncertainty.

As children of God we know who to turn to: our loving Father and our Blessed Mother Mary. Cry out to them for they are near and will journey with you and provide comfort.

PRAYER. *Mary, my mother, I beg for your loving presence and assurance of God's will.*

SOMETIMES a cup of coffee with a friend communicates all the care in the world.
—Mick Jones, M.D.

The ordinary things of life

REFLECTION. When we think of our most memorable meals they usually end up being some that we least expect: the last Thanksgiving before a relative passed away or the last time all of our childhood friends came back from school.

This meal can be very significant not for what was served but for who was present. Love and care are often served around a humble table.

PRAYER. *Jesus, as You spent time around the table with Your disciples may I share love at my meals.*

THE tenderness of God is present in the lives of all those who attend the sick and understand their needs, with eyes full of love.
—Pope Francis

You are a carrier of God's love

REFLECTION. People can look for God's presence in the heavens and through miraculous signs. While God can certainly perform the miraculous, He tends to disguise Himself in ordinary people like you and me.

We may be so close to God that we fail to see His hand on our life and His Spirit animating our actions. Where there is love, God is close by.

PRAYER. *Holy Spirit, may I be more tender in my words and actions towards others.*

FOR you Jesus, if you want it I want it too!
—Blessed Chiara Luce Badano

Total surrender to God's will

REFLECTION. Blessed Chiara was in her teens when she learned of her fatal diagnosis. A beautiful young woman with the world in front of her responded with those beautiful words. She wanted to live but surrendered all to God's will.

We, too, can learn from this young woman when we don't understand what's going on in our lives. Trust Jesus in all things.

PRAYER. *Blessed Chiara, pray for me as I surrender to God's will and care for others.*

THE biblical Abigail was beautiful but we remember her for her strength.
—Paula Matchen, Grandmother

Biblical beauty

REFLECTION. Abigail is one of the prominent women in the Bible for she acted with great courage when confronting David, the future King of Israel. While we may spend some time on our outward appearance, do we take time to work on virtue and our spiritual life.

Beauty will indeed fade but the loving care you show each day may be remembered long after you're gone.

PRAYER. *Jesus, may my inner beauty and strength be as beautiful as Abigail's.*

ANXIETY is the greatest evil that can befall a soul except sin.

—St. Francis de Sales

NOV.
20

Paralysis by analysis

REFLECTION. People who care for others are naturally in situations where life and quality of life are at stake so worry may seem natural. We must remember that Jesus, not us, is the savior of the world.

Throughout the Bible we are told, commanded even, not to worry but rather to present our needs to God through prayer. Do your best and pray through any anxiety.

PRAYER. *Jesus, I do worry and at times I'm filled with anxiety; remind me to pray often.*

GOD commands you to pray, but he forbids you to worry. —St. Francis de Sales

NOV.
21

Be consistent in prayer

REFLECTION. The quality of our faith is tested when times get tough. This is not only a reality to Catholics, but for all people, even for those without faith.

As Catholics we have a tremendous gift in our faith and through our prayer. Do you have a regular prayer time? Do you have an appointment time with God each day?

PRAYER. *Lord, may my concerns and joys reach Your Sacred Heart throughout the day.*

IF YOU don't learn to deny yourself, you can make no progress in perfection.

—St. John of the Cross

Take up your cross daily

REFLECTION. The life of Jesus reveals a life of love. Jesus never used His miraculous powers for His own benefit, but He used them for others. He who was hungry didn't feed Himself, but when He saw others hungry He multiplied the loaves and fish.

When we deny ourselves and use our gifts for the benefit of others we begin to travel the road of Christ, the road of perfection.

PRAYER. *Jesus our hope, remind me to use my gifts for the benefit of those I care for.*

LOVE our lady! She will obtain abundant grace to help you conquer in your struggles.

—St. Josemaria Escriva

Mary, be a mother to me

REFLECTION. Every Catholic Church worldwide contains an image or statue honoring our Blessed Mother. She who gave Christ to the world and nurtured Him as a youth is remembered and honored for saying "yes" to God.

In your loving service to others you are uniting your life to both Jesus and Mary who came not to be served but to serve.

PRAYER. *Mary, be a mother to me especially when I am overwhelmed and struggling.*

KEEP a clear eye towards life's end.
—St. Francis of Assisi

Eyes on the prize

REFLECTION. When running a race one can get to a point of wanting to give up. The fatigue, the hills, and exhaustion can take its toll. One thing that keeps runners going is that they have their focus on the finish line.

Our finish line is Heaven. When caring for others and giving of yourself seems fruitless remember the bigger picture and imitate Jesus who had His focus on Heaven.

PRAYER. *Humble St. Francis, may your example continue to inspire me to be all I can be.*

GIVING back to the community is what we are all called to do.
—Dr. Nathan Willard

More than a paycheck

REFLECTION. Most of us need a job in order to pay the bills and provide for our families. Catholics view their careers as more than a means to pay the bills but as an opportunity to give back to others because God has blessed them with so much.

What skills, gifts, or hobbies do you excel in which you can share with the community?

PRAYER. *Jesus, may I give back to the community with the gifts You have given me.*

UR family began to take seriously God's command to keep the Sabbath holy. —Dan Greco, Father and Coach

Rest and relaxation is important

REFLECTION. There was a time when Sunday's were reserved for God and family time. Today there are pressures to give that time away to shopping and sports.

How can you begin to take back Sunday? Start with something small like a family brunch after Mass. Remember God commands it because He knows it will be good for us and our family.

PRAYER. *Lord, may my family start to take back Sunday to honor You and enjoy each other.*

 EVER underestimate the power of a positive word or remembering a name. —Nancy Richards, R.N.

Words have great power to heal and connect

REFLECTION. I was visiting a nursing home where a very elderly religious sister had retired to and in the community room there were another ten sisters gathered.

As I was leaving a sister who was in a wheelchair gently said to me, "Thank you, Allan." I don't remember being introduced to her, but her words of gratitude struck me to the core. Be generous with your words.

PRAYER. *Lord, Your words are Spirit and Life. May my words be like Yours.*

BELIEVE in one God, the Father Almighty. **NOV.**
—Nicene Creed
28

What may set us apart from others

REFLECTION. The most powerful idea that Catholics believe is said each time we recite our Creed. As faithful Catholics we may take these words for granted, but there are many people who do not share our beliefs.

We do believe in God not just as the creator but as Father and friend. With this belief we may have a different view of the world and of our purpose which is a good thing.

PRAYER. *Lord, may I never waver in my belief that You are present and that You love me.*

O MATTER what Catholic Church I **NOV.**
attend I feel at home.
—Karl Hungus, Pediatrician
29

There's no place like home

REFLECTION. It can be interesting to attend Mass in another parish or especially in a foreign country. While there may be a difference in language or local tradition the Catholic Church has some common elements no matter where we attend.

We can be assured of statues of Mary and St. Joseph, the Word of God being proclaimed, and most importantly the celebration of the Most Holy Eucharist.

PRAYER. *Jesus, may You make Your home in my heart through the Eucharist.*

N O ACT of caring is ever wasted.
—Jack Fagan, Teacher

It all matters to God

REFLECTION. The last few minutes of a lopsided sports victory is often called "garbage time." Coaches will try to get players in the game who don't play often because the victory is assured.

To God, there is no "garbage time" in our life. Every act of caring in every moment counts. Seek opportunities to serve and you will be surprised what a difference it can make.

PRAYER. *Lord, I offer You my loving service through those You place in my life.*

REMEMBER that the Lord wonderfully favors those who are faithful. —Ps 4:4

Faithfulness, not success

REFLECTION. While our motivation for serving should come from a heart filled with the love of God, we sometimes wonder if God notices. Yes, He does! Not only does God notice but He assures us that we will receive His love and favor.

Rewards are nice but the knowledge that we are doing God's will surpasses any temporal gifts we may receive. Focus on being faithful.

PRAYER. *Lord, may I serve You out of a heart filled with gratitude.*

FOR only with your help. O Lord, can I rest secure. —Ps 4:9

DEC.
2

In Him we rest assured

REFLECTION. We all have issues and people in our lives that can keep us awake at night. It was no different in biblical times. While others rely on us for our care and loving service we have a great God who cares for us.

Leave the worries of the day with Him, place them at His feet and get some sleep. The Lord of the universe is on your side and desires that you rest assured.

PRAYER. *Lord, I cast my cares upon You for I know You care for me.*

LORD, at daybreak you hear my voice. —Ps 5:4

DEC.
3

When does the Lord hear from you?

REFLECTION. It would seem that the author of the Psalms had a regular time for praying. Having a regular prayer time has been a part of the Judeo-Christian tradition for centuries.

God knows that we can be forgetful, so if we don't have a specific time each day we can tend to forget to pray. When is the best time for you to pray? At daybreak or nightfall? While commuting or waiting at the supermarket?

PRAYER. *Lord, may I commit to a regular time of prayer each day.*

WILL sing hymns of praise to the name of the Lord Most High. —Ps 7:18

DEC.

4

Express yourself in song!

REFLECTION. People love music and they love to sing. The next time you're walking down the street or at the gym, check out how many people have their earbuds in and are listening to music.

Have you considered music as a way of praising God? Invest in some uplifting Christian music and have the words of praise and thanksgiving on your lips as you give praise to God.

PRAYER. *Jesus, may I offer You my heart and express my love to You in song.*

———————————

 LORD, our Lord, how glorious is your name in all the earth! —Ps 8:10

DEC.

5

The name of God has power

REFLECTION. I find it strange and somewhat amusing that at the name of God even the most staunch atheists become instant theologians. The name of Jesus has power to save and it also can stir up some controversy for those who do not believe.

In your service to others never be afraid to speak the name of Jesus, or if you can, pray with people. His name still has power to save.

PRAYER. *Lord, may I never be ashamed of Your name or my faith in You.*

O NOT forget the afflicted. —Ps 10:12 **DEC.**

6

God will use you in a powerful way

REFLECTION. There are many ways to be afflicted in this life. We see physical, psychological, and emotional afflictions as but a few of the ways that people are afflicted today.

You, through your care and support, are an instrument of God's love. Thank you for the sacrifices you have made in bringing God's comfort to others who are afflicted in many ways. You are a gift!

PRAYER. *Loving Father, may I bring Your love to others through my everyday actions.*

ELP, O Lord, for there are no godly left. **DEC.**
—Ps 12:2

7

When you feel alone in service

REFLECTION. St. John wrote that the light shines in the darkness and the darkness does not overcome it, early on in his Gospel. We can and do feel overwhelmed at times when it seems that God is far from us and that we are the only one left who believes.

The author of the Psalms felt comfortable crying out to God for help and so should we. Be honest in your prayer and petitions.

PRAYER. *Lord, help me never to lose faith and hope in Your loving care for me.*

WILL sing to the Lord for he has been good to me. —Ps 13:7

Sing in the midst of sorrow

REFLECTION. Psalm 13 is titled, Prayer of One in Sorrow. When we come to the last line however we read that the Psalmist will sing to the Lord. Have you ever thanked God in advance for what He will do in your life?

In the midst of sorrow, the author of the Psalms sings not because things are bad but because he knows the goodness and love of God. You have good reason to sing.

PRAYER. *Mary, Mother of God, may I trust in God's will as you did and sing of His goodness.*

 Y STEPS have held fast to your paths; my feet have not wavered. —Ps 17:5

Trust the process, trust God's word

REFLECTION. Athletes are called to trust the process that their coaches provide for them. They may not understand why the coach has them complete a set of exercises or routines but they complete them due to trust in their coach.

When God calls us to stay close to Him and to obey His word we may not understand why but we trust that He knows what is best for us. Stay the course!

PRAYER. *Holy Spirit, convict my heart when I have strayed so I may return to God.*

T. PETER committed one of the greatest sins, denying Christ, and yet they made him pope. Think about that.

—Pope Francis

God's mercy is boundless

REFLECTION. How often do we focus on our own sinfulness instead of God's boundless mercy? Yes, we acknowledge and confess our sins but do we leave them with God's mercy or do we carry them with us?

St. Peter was a better person and leader because he learned from his past sins and so should all of us. Never let your sins keep you from caring and moving forward in faith.

PRAYER. *Loving Lord, thank You for Your limitless mercy.*

 OR in truth we are not called only once, but many times throughout our life.

—Cardinal John Henry Newman

Attuned to His voice

REFLECTION. We may be able to identify the first time our faith really meant something to us or when we became serious about following Jesus. We may identify that time as God calling us to Himself and it can be a turning point for many.

The truth is that God never stops calling us to go deeper in our relationship with Him. Be open to God's ongoing call in your life.

PRAYER. *Lord, speak, Your servant is listening for Your call in their life.*

179

T HE commands of the Lord are clear, giving light to the eyes. —Ps 19:9

Easy to follow directions

REFLECTION. To those who have faith and have been given a good education the commands of the Lord are indeed clear. "Love one another," "Forgive seventy times seven," and "Do unto others as you would have them do unto you" are easy to understand. Living them out is another matter.

Imagine how the world is a little different because you have the faith to live these out.

PRAYER. *Jesus, may my faithfulness to Your word be my gift to You.*

W E ARE not meant to live for ourselves alone, but for God and others. —Bishop Arthur J. Serratelli

What are you building?

REFLECTION. Jesus was a carpenter yet we don't have anything that He ever built. While the kings in Jesus' day named cities and buildings after themselves, Jesus renamed people and built them up.

Our legacy will not be in buildings which will in time crumble, but in people! Invest time and energy in building others up and there you will see God's Kingdom.

PRAYER. *Lord God, may each loving action I perform be a brick in building Your kingdom.*

REGRET all the time I wasted using others to my own end.

— Eugene Anoest, Construction engineer

DEC. 14

Use your time well

REFLECTION. Learning from the mistakes of others can be a source of great wisdom and can direct our own steps as we follow Christ in our lives.

A selfish heart seeks only glory and honor for itself and will use others to accomplish this. A Christian heart, one attuned to the Holy Spirit, will seek to work with others for a common goal.

PRAYER. *Jesus, may my intentions be pure in all that You call me to in serving others.*

HY did I make a habit of spending 15 hours a day at work and neglect my wife and child?

— Dennis Asinu

DEC. 15

What are your priorities?

REFLECTION. Caregivers are called by their very nature to sacrifice time and energy for others, but they should not neglect their family. We may think that we are so needed by others that we forget the vows we made when we married.

Spend time and plan time with your family for that is your primary vocation as husband or wife. You will not regret it later in life.

PRAYER. *Blessed Mother, may I be present to my spouse and children as you were.*

AY he give you your heart's desire and grant you success in all your plans. —Ps 20:5

He desires our success

REFLECTION. When things are going good some people just wait for the "other shoe to drop" because they think God is going to ruin their success for some odd reason. This line of thinking is not of God!

God desires our best and wants our success even more than we do. Reflect on your heart's desire and present your needs to Him for He wants to be part of the solution.

PRAYER. *Loving God, may the desires of my heart be placed in Your Sacred Heart.*

 DIDN'T realize how bitter I was until someone confronted me. —Ginger Zamen, Clerk

Who can speak honestly to you?

REFLECTION. Unfortunately, many people who harbor bitterness and resentment never realize how it affects them. Sin can blind us to our own faults, so we need people in our lives who can gently let us know of our negative behavior.

Having the humility to realize our own faults and working to improve ourselves is a step in being free and will allow us to serve joyfully.

PRAYER. *Lord, may I have the humility to accept criticism and the desire to grow as a person.*

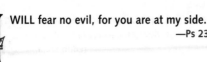

WILL fear no evil, for you are at my side.
—Ps 23:4

The Lord walks beside us

REFLECTION. The Scripture is clear that there is evil in the world. Anyone with eyes and ears can identify how evil manifests itself in our world. As Catholics, we are called to resist evil and do good, be good, and be a power for good.

While evil may be all around us we move forward in following Jesus' way of love because He is at our side each step of the way.

PRAYER. *Lord, let me follow You wherever You lead me.*

FOUND that any act of caring has a ripple effect.
—Maureen Foley, Teacher

Be a ripple maker

REFLECTION. Like a paper airplane that gets thrown into a summer breeze we never know what our actions of caring will lead to.

Not only can the action itself have ripple effects, but think about your witness to others who may be watching you care for others. You may be the example that others may follow. Be generous in all of your actions of love.

PRAYER. *Jesus, help me not to miss moments each day where I can show care and concern.*

GOD does all things at the right time.

—St. Teresa Benedicta of the Cross
(Edith Stein)

DEC.
20

Be faithful and leave the rest to God

REFLECTION. God's timing is a lesson that many biblical characters had to learn. We can drive ourselves crazy if we think God should act on our timetable and waste precious time worrying about what God should do.

Still yourself. Do the small things with love, and you will learn that God does all things at the right time.

PRAYER. *Jesus, increase my trust in You and in Your timing.*

BEAR one another's burdens, and in this way you will fulfill the law of Christ.

—Gal 6:2

DEC.
21

Love in action

REFLECTION. They say that it's not the cross we bear but how we bear it that makes all the difference. As caregivers we carry our own cross and assist countless people in helping them with their crosses.

When we can see the face of Jesus in the face of those we serve we will be able to serve with joy. Where have you seen the face of Jesus this week?

PRAYER. *St. Paul, pray for me that I may bear my burden well.*

E CARE for others because He first cared for us. —Sr. Assunta Flannery

Jesus is our model

REFLECTION. Catholics stand at the beginning of Mass when the Word of God is processed in with song. The Scriptures reveal to us the living Word of God and how we should imitate Christ.

Following Jesus may not always be valued by those around you but we know that following Christ is the way that leads to life. Model your life on the life of the Master.

PRAYER. *St. Joseph, pray for me that I may serve as you and Christ did.*

T. JOSEPH is a man without words but not without witness. —A. Frederick Wright

St. Joseph, Patron of the Universal Church

REFLECTION. When you are a person of honor you don't need many words. St. Joseph was such a man. He showed a costly demonstration of unexpected love to his wife and child from the moment the angel spoke to him.

Who has demonstrated caring and loving actions in your life? In what areas of your life can you be more of a person of action?

PRAYER. *St. Joseph, may you be a role model to me as I serve even without a lot of words.*

BUT the angel said to them, "Do not be afraid, for I bring you good news of great joy for all the people." —Lk 2:10

God came for all of us

REFLECTION. The Good News of Jesus was announced to lowly shepherds who were out in their fields tending their sheep. While we might expect this news to be shared first with the wealthy and powerful, God acts through ordinary and at times unexpected people.

Be open to being used by God and never be afraid to bring His love and care to all people that you encounter.

PRAYER. *My guardian angel, guide me and pray for me that I may not be afraid to serve.*

———————

THE Church's vocation is to bring joy to the world, a joy that is authentic and enduring. —Pope Benedict XVI

The mission of the Church continues

REFLECTION. On this day the Church remembers the Incarnation, Christmas, the day that God became one of us. God so loved you and me that He humbled Himself and took on human flesh in order to communicate His love in a way that we could see, hear, touch, and understand.

This mission of love continues through the Church, through you and me.

PRAYER. *Mary, Mother of Jesus, pray for us who continue the mission of Jesus, a mission of love.*

HIS mother treasured all these things in her heart.
—Lk 2:51

DEC.
26

What do you treasure?

REFLECTION. We are told that Mary treasured many things in her heart and no doubt that St. Joseph was on the top of her list. Here is a man who loved her, protected her, and was obedient to the Word of God.

What or rather who do you treasure in your own heart? Take time to thank God for them and if you can, let them know you treasure them.

PRAYER. *Lord, may I be more grateful for those who love me and care for me.*

YOU are witnesses to all these things.
—Lk 24:48

DEC.
27

Be a light for others

REFLECTION. At the end of the Gospel of Luke we read these words stating that "you are witnesses to these things." Like the shepherds at the beginning of the Gospel we all have a responsibility to be a witness to the life and love of Jesus Christ.

Reflect on your encounter with Jesus and the positive difference it has made in your life. Share this witness with others.

PRAYER. *Lord, may I decrease and Your presence within me increase.*

WE CANNOT keep ourselves shut up in parishes, in our communities, when so many people are waiting for the Gospel!

DEC. 28

—Pope Francis

Receive and then give

REFLECTION. Few Catholics have experienced faith-sharing in the home while growing up. We are familiar with prayer, going to Mass, and too often leaving faith-sharing to the priests and religious.

Break the culture of silence! At home and when you are out in the world share your love for Jesus for without this the faith will fade and souls will be lost.

PRAYER. *Lord, what You ask is challenging but I know You go before me always.*

———————

INTENSE love doesn't measure, it just gives.

DEC. 29

—St. Teresa of Calcutta

Don't count the cost

REFLECTION. When it comes to love our ultimate example is Jesus. He gave all for us—emptying Himself and becoming one of us and then dying for us on the Cross. He continues to give Himself to us through the Eucharist.

How do we respond to such love? By giving our all through love, caring, and service.

PRAYER. *Jesus, give me Your joy in giving all in love.*

IVE thanks to the Lord, for he is good; his kindness endures forever.

—Ps 118:1

DEC. 30

It is right to give Him thanks and praise

REFLECTION. The root of the word we use for "kindness" is "kin," which is used for family. While Jesus is Lord and God in the flesh, He considers us family.

What a gift it is to be welcomed into the family of God! What a joy to count God as our Father and others as our brothers and sisters. Take time to thank God and time just to be in His presence.

PRAYER. *Lord, thank You for welcoming me into Your family of faith.*

 EE, I am making all things new.

—Rev 21:5

DEC. 31

An end and a beginning

REFLECTION. With a new year ahead of us we have an opportunity to review the past year with its challenges and successes. We can also recommit ourselves to whatever goals we wish to accomplish or actions we wish to improve upon.

We do not know what the new year may bring, but we are assured of God's love and presence as we move forward in faith.

PRAYER. *Jesus, be with me and my loved ones as we follow You, and grant us Your peace.*

Prayer of Lay People

HEAVENLY Father,
help me to exercise my lay apostolate
where I work or practice my profession,
or study or reside,
or spend any leisure time
or have my companionships.
Grant that I may become the light of the world
by conforming my life to my faith.
By practicing honesty in all my dealings,
may I attract all whom I meet
to the love of the true and the good,
and ultimately to the Church and to Christ.
Inspire me to share in the living conditions
as well as the labors, sorrows, and aspirations
of my brothers and sisters,
thus preparing their hearts
for the worship of Your saving grace.
Enable me to perform
my domestic, social, and professional duties
with such Christian generosity
that my way of acting will penetrate
the world of life and labor.
Teach me to cooperate
with all men and women of goodwill
in promoting whatever is true,
whatever is just,
whatever is holy, and whatever is lovable.
Let me complement the testimony of life
with the testimony of the word,
so that I will proclaim Christ
to those brothers and sisters
who can hear the Gospel
through no one else except me.

Prayer of Law Enforcers

HEAVENLY Father,
You have created a marvelous world
that is permeated by a wondrous sense of order.
Yet human beings have a tendency
to war against order on their level.
That is the reason why there are people like me
who work at maintaining order in society.
Help me to use my authority with understanding
and restraint
and without bias or anger.
Let me remember that in carrying out my function
I am sharing in your Divine Providence in the
universe
so that the people in this world can live full lives
and grow in the knowledge and love of You,
of Your Son, and of the Holy Spirit.

Prayer of Members of the Armed Forces

O LORD,
You are the God of hosts.
Strengthen us who are members
of our country's armed forces.
Make us prepare so well to defend our country
that we will eliminate the need to do so.
In serving our superiors
may we be rendering service to You.
Make us loyal to our loved ones
in spite of separations of every kind.
Keep us devoted to Your Church
in spite of the pressures of our duties.
Help us to lead others to You
by the example we give to our comrades-in-arms.

Prayer for a Loving Attitude

LORD Jesus Christ,
You gave Your life out of love for all people
and You encouraged Your followers to do good to
others.
Over the years many Christians have found this
difficult,
and I am no exception.
I try, but it is so hard
to have a loving attitude toward all—
and then I feel hypocritical in claiming to follow
You.
Help me, dear Lord, to really believe
that Christian love is the greatest energy in the
world.
Let me see that this is not an emotion
but a central attitude of one's being—
an attitude of service for others in Your Name.
It is the result of Your grace,
and prompts us to will only good things for others
as images of God.
Grant that I may always strive to attain this attitude
and so live up to the noble vocation to which I
am called.